Mindfulness for a Happy Life

Mindfulness for a Happy Life

New Teachings of an Old Tradition for Today's World

Robert Beatty

with Laura Musikanski

Foreword by Paige Cogger

RESOURCE *Publications* · Eugene, Oregon

MINDFULNESS FOR A HAPPY LIFE
New Teachings of an Old Tradition for Today's World

Resource Publications
An Imprint of Wipf and Stock Publishers
199 W. 8th Ave., Suite 3
Eugene, OR 97401

www.wipfandstock.com

PAPERBACK ISBN: 978-1-5326-7367-2
HARDCOVER ISBN: 978-1-5326-7368-9
EBOOK ISBN: 978-1-5326-7369-6

Manufactured in the U.S.A.   06/19/20

Almost fifty years ago when I encountered Buddhism and meditation it was clear to me that I wanted to devote my life to waking up and helping others along. This book is dedicated to Ruth Denison, my Dharma mother and teacher, who opened my heart and mind.

Contents

Foreword

I ARRIVED FOR ROBERT Beatty's five-day retreat already having had many years of meditation experience. I had studied Buddhism in Sri Lanka while living at a meditation center and had attended countless retreats, consisting mostly of the traditional "sit, walk, sit" format. I still attached, though subtly, to the idea of myself as a "serious and experienced meditator."

I made my way to the Dharma hall, placed my cushion in what felt like just the right spot and sat myself down. Sitting quietly, I awaited Robert's arrival. I had yet to meet him, and I was curious.

He entered the room with gusto. A kind and lighthearted playfulness exuded from him. I found this to be incredibly refreshing and comforting. It also left me doubting, questioning: "Who is this guy? Is this going to be a 'serious' Insight Meditation retreat?"

Indeed, Robert had a thorough understanding of and experience with the traditional approach and discipline of sitting and walking meditation. Instruction was offered in clear and accessible ways. Much time was given for the formal and classical style of practice. In addition to this, Robert invited and encouraged us to explore movement, to dance, to listen to sounds and to music with fresh ears, and to take in the beauty of the natural world. He honored the importance of joy and acknowledged the truth of the vulnerable and emotional state of the human condition. Time was given to share, to connect and to be with one another.

For me, this was a whole new style of meditation retreat. I was, at first, a bit shocked, but rather quickly, Robert's teaching style helped me see the ways I had been hiding. I began to see more clearly how dangerously skillful I had become at compartmentalizing. Yes, I could sit for hours, and yes, I had benefited deeply from these past retreats and knowledgeable teachers. Still, the integration piece had been quite rocky. The return home often left me a bit shaky, with some nervous energy and a level of sensitivity that at times had me subtly seeking out ways to numb. The transition from retreat time to life at home had been a tough one for me. I do not think I am alone in this.

Robert's style of teaching has and continues to help me bring the Dharma more fully into all parts of my life. In countless ways, both through his formal teachings and the lessons that shine through his living example, Robert helps me to rest in a place of greater kindness, patience, generosity and joy with myself and the world around me. This has been and continues to be the precious gift that Robert's style of teaching brings to me and so many.

Robert supports and encourages a kind and courageous allowing of the experiences of pain *and* a courageous opening up to and participation in the experiences of joy. He generously offers the classical teachings of the Buddha and Theravada Buddhism with great respect and knowledge. This is done in a way that is so very helpful, accessible and applicable in our often busy modern lives (and all the varied moods and mind states that come and go with it!). We are given the classical teachings without dogma or rigidity and we are encouraged to relax into a place of authentic spontaneity without it feeling ungrounded.

It has been said that there is no greater gift than the Dharma. With this I agree. Robert offers us this great gift of the Dharma in a unique and special way that expresses understanding and empathy for the human condition with all its ups and downs. Robert's skillful and genuine style of being and teaching helps me and so many live life with more ease, joy, acceptance and kindness. This book brings the great gift of even more accessibility to Robert's teachings, and with this, greater opportunities for deep healing and genuine happiness.

Again and again, I bow with gratitude to you Robert, my beloved teacher and Dharma friend. Thank you.

Paige Cogger is a yoga and meditation teacher in the Ruth Denison lineage working and living in Ashland, Oregon.

Preface

ROBERT BEATTY CHANGED MY life. His talks are so moving, real and vulnerable that they cut through my deep resolve never to have anything to do with any religion, least of all Buddhism. When I first approached Robert to write a book based on his talks, his response was, "Sure, but others have tried." By that time, I had listened to hundreds of hours of his talks posted to YouTube between 2010 and 2015. Many of them are now gone due to a YouTube snafu when the name of the station was changed to *Robert Beatty & PIMC* (a lesson in impermanence!). I set to work.

Some chapters are taken entirely from one talk, and others, such as the one on the five hindrances, are compilations of six or seven talks. The chapters began as transcripts of the talks. Then, I reorganized each chapter because the logical flow of talking does not always make sense in print. At times, a half phrase or hint at a concept was not covered in a talk. I had spent enough time on retreats with Robert to fill gaps from memory. In a few places I brought in the work on happiness and well-being that I have been doing since 2010. The chapters evolved as Robert and I worked together on Zoom meetings, reading each sentence aloud and carefully editing the manuscripts. We went back and forth over each chapter, imagining you, the reader, with us, as if we were in the same room. Robert's teachings are lively, and often involve imagined conversations with the Buddha or actual interactions with Robert's students and followers. Throughout the book, we used italics instead of quotation marks, so you will see where he is speaking with you as if you were in the room with him. In the final stages of writing this book, Robert asked several of his friends, students and two professional editors to read through the manuscript. All along the way, the intent was to capture the beauty and truth of Robert's teachings. They are not perfect. In their imperfection is their beauty and their truth. That is one reason his teachings reached me, and, I hope, you, dear reader.

It has taken over four years to write this book and too many hours to count. The book captures the essence of Robert's teachings, but more importantly, is an approach to Buddhism that is needed today. There are probably hundreds or thousands of books on Buddhism and mindfulness. *Mindfulness for a Happy Life* is like no other because of the way that Robert teaches. He is open and honest about what it means to live the everyday life, and he is wise and compassionate about how to apply the lessons of Buddhism to everyday life events. He does not pretend that he has no skeletons in his closet. Instead, he pulls them out, and in doing so, frees us to be present to the shadows and skeletons in our own closets that keep us from waking up. He does not pretend that life will miraculously get easier or better if you meditate just right. Instead, he helps you develop the skills for living a life with love and compassion, even as life gives its inevitable blows and losses. I am deeply grateful for the opportunity to write this book with Robert, to get to know his teachings so intimately, and to learn the Dharma through his teachings. I believe in him, and I hope that what he says will touch you as well.

Laura Musikanski
Happiness Alliance

Acknowledgements

THE SEEDS OF THIS book germinated in India almost half a century ago. It was there that I encountered a world so different from my own that I was forced to question my view of reality. I bow to Mother India.

I am profoundly grateful to Laura Musikanski. Almost five years ago she approached me with a plan to create a book from the talks I had given while teaching retreats. She worked tirelessly, listening, transcribing and bringing order to the ideas. We touched and worked every page together. This book would not have come to fruition without her support and encouragement.

I have been nourished along the way by many Dharma teachers, each of whom helped to shape my understanding of the path and the opening of my heart. I bow to: S N Goenka, Sujata, Jack Kornfield, Anagarika Munindra, Joanna Macy, Stephen Levine, Joseph Goldstein and Matt Flicktstein.

Another thread of profound nourishment to which I bow is the line of wise and loving psychotherapists who have graced my life over many decades. They helped me face into the psychological trauma and wounds of my childhood, and helped me integrate Western psychology with the teachings of the Buddha. I bow to them and in particular: Don Nickerson, Tad Achord, Anita Witt, Ann Kafoury, Shelley Hanson, and David Bice.

I bow deeply in gratitude to the thousands of students who have attended my classes, retreats and countless individual meetings and shared the vulnerable and precious experiences of their healing and awakening with me. All along the way we have been learning from each other.

I am grateful to Ann Greenberger and Murray Reiss for their significant editorial contributions. Beyond them this book had been loved, edited, read and shaped by so many hearts that I am concerned that if I begin to mention specific persons, I will create suffering by omitting important contributors. As you read this please know that you are part of it. I bow to you in gratitude.

Finally, I want to thank my wife Jennifer Leddy for her loving support and for being my partner in the dance of relationship and awakening.

Introduction

You hold in your hands a book that could radically change your life. It's a book about waking up from the trance of everyday life and becoming more fully alive. It contains a modern interpretation of a path to happiness that human beings have followed for almost 2,600 years. I have been on this path for five decades and have shared intimately in the journeys of thousands of my students and clients as they too have turned inward in meditation.

This is a book about practice and taking responsibility for your own mind, emotions and actions. You will be encouraged to go beyond theory, thinking and interesting ideas and to really look inside unflinchingly. You will be guided to sit down to meditate and to bring mindfulness into every single activity of your life. You will discover what mindfulness really is. If you practice, the revolutionary phenomenon of mindfulness will transform your life and you will experience a quiet happiness for which you have always longed.

Countless people have tried to meditate and have quit because they did not receive proper instruction or support. They believed that to succeed they needed to stop their mind from wandering and enter a state of silent bliss. They anticipated exotic states and out-of-body experiences. While such phenomena do exist, they are not signs of spiritual development or of skillful practice. Instead, what is needed is great patience and a willingness to experience and open to whatever life presents, to bring love and open-hearted acceptance into every aspect of your life.

Every human life is difficult and utterly unpredictable. From birth to death we are presented with experiences that oscillate from pleasant to unpleasant in a heartbeat.

Introduction

Ever since the Big Bang everything in our universe has been in constant change. Each of us is born, appearing out of nowhere, lives a lifetime and then disappears. Between the dramatic beginning and ending we experience a kaleidoscopic flow of experiences. Nothing stays the same. We are healthy then sick, life is easy then difficult, relationships begin and end. To the degree that we deny the radical impermanence of everything, we suffer and cause others to suffer. When we wake up to this we learn how to live more happily and to navigate the river of our lives more wisely.

The practice of mindfulness allows you to really embrace the truth of your life. Awakening to this truth will allow you to diminish how much unnecessary suffering you create. You will learn to live in the vibrant aliveness of the present moment where life really happens.

This path of waking up lies wide open before you. All you need to do is open up to it. I hope this book will be a doorway for you to set off on your own inner journey with the tools you need and the inspiration to develop them.

1

Introduction to Mindfulness and the Path to Happiness

You carry all the ingredients
To turn existence into joy,
Mix them,
mix
them!

—HAFIZ

The human mind can be your best friend
and worst enemy.

—*BHAGAVAD GITA*

Mindfulness: The Path to Happiness

RIGHT NOW, YOU HAVE within you the potential for true happiness. You can realize it through the practice of mindfulness, the mysterious phenomenon of awareness. This miracle of awakeness is available to everybody in every moment.

Perhaps you have tried to meditate in the past and have given up because you felt defeated by the out-of-control nature of your mind. You believed that you had to stop your mind and that to be successful you had to feel bliss. I invite you to try meditation again with a different intention. Let go of the idea of doing it perfectly. Instead, become very curious. Look upon your meditation as a journey of exploration and discovery of the most important person in your world: you.

Join me in a simple experiment.

Become aware that you are seeing.

Did you notice the shift? A moment ago, there was seeing, but now there is knowing that there is seeing. How did that happen? How did you do it? There was no thunderbolt of lightning that brought awareness. It was not as if the clouds parted and everything started to glitter. An awareness of seeing arose. Just that.

If you can know that seeing is happening, you can also be aware of hearing, tasting and touching. You can be aware that thinking is happening. You can know that emotion is happening. This knowing is mindfulness. This capacity of awareness of your life experience is the doorway to freedom.

With the practice of mindfulness, you develop your capacity for balance in the face of hardship. When strong feelings arise, a memory is stirred up, an old pattern is triggered or a biological impulse is sparked, you learn how to become aware of their arising and can make skillful choices that are loving, compassionate and beneficial for yourself and others. The life of blind reactivity slowly fades away.

If you begin to practice mindfulness today and practice every day for a week or month, it is very likely that at some point, even if only for a brief moment, you will find you are not at the whim of something that usually triggers you. It may not last long, and you may go right back into your habitual behaviors, but that moment is the beginning of awakening. Over time, you will develop your ability to watch your personality unfold. You will learn how to restrain unskillful actions that leave a wake of unhappiness in your life. You will begin to cultivate skillful actions, that leave a wake of ease and happiness for yourself and others.

What Is Mindfulness?

Mindfulness is one of the great mysteries of human life. It is our capacity to be aware of being aware. Buddha discovered that this aspect of consciousness can be cultivated and is the key we can use to set ourselves free from suffering.

There is a huge change in the life of someone who begins to practice mindfulness. With just a bit of practice we notice how out of control the mind really is. We begin to be able to observe thoughts, feelings and emotions as experiences that we are having rather than identifying with them. To see thoughts and emotions like anger, sadness, fear and worry as objective phenomena rather than as oneself is radically liberating.

My introduction to mindfulness took place in Bodh Gaya, India, in 1971. This is where Buddha experienced his awakening. In the days following the retreat, I saw a batik on the wall of a small shop that stopped me in my tracks. The eyes in the background summarized the entire teachings for me. It was dusty and not for sale, but I asked the shopkeeper if I could buy it. With some reticence, he let me purchase it. Today, almost fifty years later, it hangs on the west wall of the meditation hall of the Portland Insight Meditation Center. It is an elegant representation of the most profound truth.

The image depicts four elements of the awakening journey. In the foreground is Buddha blessing a mindfulness practitioner. This symbolizes the beginning of the journey to awakening. Encompassing this image is a sitting Buddha, symbolizing the practice of meditation. Containing these two images is Buddha standing, representing the teachings and the practicing of them in all the activities of daily life. Beyond these three images are two eyes. The eyes represent the mystery of awareness. No matter what is happening there is a capacity in human consciousness to be aware of it and not identify with it. No matter what we are experiencing, whether pleasant or unpleasant, it is always possible to step into awareness and to not identify with the experience. This is what is called freedom in Buddhism. This capacity of simple awareness is realized through the practice of mindfulness.

What Draws People to Mindfulness

There are a number of reasons people begin to practice mindfulness.

One is stress management. Another is a desire to reduce suffering and to experience increased psychological and emotional well-being. A third reason is the quest to answer the fundamental spiritual question, *Who am I?* Mindfulness practice has brought happiness to countless people by serving these three functions and many more.

No matter what draws you, mindfulness begins as meditation practice. This practice is an exercise for the mind. Just as you can exercise to strengthen particular physical muscles, you can do exercises to strengthen mental muscles. In mindfulness practice we work to strengthen two specific mental factors: mindfulness and concentration.

Mindfulness of breathing is an excellent practice to begin your meditation journey. With this practice you sit comfortably upright and bring awareness to the physical sensations of breathing in and out. You may bring attention to the sensation in the chest and abdomen, or to the feeling of the air as it comes in and out of the nose. You set your intention to notice the beginning of the breath, at the inhale, and then follow it through until the end of the exhale. This is more easily said than done. For most of us, the mind wanders off halfway through the first or second breath. After a few seconds or minutes, awareness that the mind has wandered arises, and then we bring our focus back to the breath. Every time you bring your focus back, it is for the mind like pumping iron is for the muscles. You strengthen your capacity to be aware, concentrated and content.

Mindfulness Basics: When the Mind Runs Out of Control (Which It Will)

If every time you sat down to meditate, you experienced great ease and happiness, you would not have any trouble establishing a daily practice. Meditation would be an immediate ultimate vacation. If this were the case, everybody would meditate.

For most people, however, it's the opposite. They may have heard about mindfulness from a friend or seen courses offered at work or in their neighborhood. They try to meditate and then quickly quit because they don't know what to expect or how to deal with what happens. They have no idea how much the mind wanders. They believe that all their thoughts and feelings define who they are. With nothing to distract them from those thoughts and feelings, and nothing to do about them, they get overwhelmed. They do not know that it is natural and normal for the mind to wander, and that the act of bringing the mind back to the breath after it wanders off is an important part of meditating.

The human mind is by nature busy and full of desire, restlessness, negativity and worry. What most people experience when they practice breath meditation, or any other kind of meditation, is a sense of constant failure. It goes like this: there is an awareness of the breath going in, then the breath going out, and then, *whoosh*. The mind goes on a trip, you fall into a trance, and thoughts consume you: *I should have checked my email before I sat down; when is he going to reply? Aaargh, why do I keep getting in these situations? Oh, no, I forgot my sister's birthday—again! I can't ever get anything right.*

The mind runs on, out of control.

Why am I so fat? I wish I could just stop eating so much. Why don't I exercise more? Darn, still need to file the taxes. Ugh, this feels terrible.

The mind is out of control.

Then the miracle happens. Out of nowhere, there is suddenly awareness that the mind is wandering. This is mindfulness. By waking up to the wandering mind, a moment of freedom arises, and you get to choose what the mind does next. That moment of freedom gives you a moment of choice, and you can choose to bring your focus back to the breath. With practice, this choice, this act, strengthens your capacity for mindfulness and concentration. Over time, this repeated experience of awareness opens the door to the realization that you are not your thoughts or your emotions.

This becomes a turning point in your life. Cultivating this awareness is the road to freedom and the path to happiness.

Right now, you can sit for five minutes and notice that your mind wanders. The wandering may happen for a tenth of a second or the entire five minutes before you notice that it is wandering. It does not matter. What matters is that there was no awareness of the fact that the mind wandered, and then awareness of wandering arose. I invite you stop reading and try it.

Wage No War Against Yourself

You may have had the experience of trying hard to concentrate on the breath, saying to yourself, *I am going to be with my breath.* Maybe you succeed for two or three minutes, five or ten minutes. Then all hell breaks loose. The mind starts to do its thing. It falls asleep or the internal mental chatter is so intense that it feels louder than a rock 'n' roll concert. You become consumed with plans for the future or obsessed with something that happened in the past. Then, you notice the mind wandering and at some point you say to yourself, *Rats! I'm not doing it right. What is wrong with me? I should try harder.*

When this happens, you can notice your self-criticism and judgment in the same way you noticed the wandering mind. You might say to yourself, instead, *Oh . . . there is that judging mind, and now I set my intention to focus on the breath.* Each time you become aware that your mind has wandered, and you bring awareness back to your breath, instead of chastising yourself for a wandering mind, congratulate yourself! Most people don't understand that the act of bringing awareness back to your breath is the most profound intervention you can make. Now you do!

Kindness, compassion and love are central to training the mind. Mindfulness practice is rooted in nonviolence. Violence is impractical. It simply does not work. It does not work in raising our kids. It does not work to improve society. It does not work for the wellness of our minds. Chastising yourself for not practicing mindfulness the right way, for the mind wandering, for falling asleep during meditation or not being able to follow your breath is a kind of violence and is based on a misunderstanding of what mindfulness is and how to practice it.

Mindfulness Will Change Your Life

If you sit in meditation for fifteen minutes focusing on your breath, and five, ten, or twenty times you bring your mind back to your breath, that would be fantastic. The arising of awareness of the wandering mind and the act of bringing your mind back to your breath is *the* intervention that leads to happiness.

If you practice fifteen or twenty minutes a day for a month, you will experience a difference in your life. For one, you will notice how absolutely crazy the mind is. We all think of the mind as *my mind*. We take it very seriously. We think we are defined by our minds. This identification with the mind combined with its craziness can make us miserable. With daily practice, we come to see that the mind does its own thing. It gets mad. It gets joyous. It gets depressed. It gets anxious. It has desires. It plans. It fantasizes. It believes it is grand. It believes it is stupid. You will start to see that what the mind does is, in a way, impersonal. You will see that, with awareness, your capacity for making choices that are helpful increases, as does a sense of ease. With these experiences, you will start to enjoy more happiness.

How Much Effort Is Too Much?

In your practice, the question will arise, *If I am taking the breath as my training object, and the mind wanders, and then I am noticing that, and then I come home to the breath, how hard should I try to come home to the breath? How much effort do I use? How much concentration do I introduce?*

There is the classic story of a monk who comes to the Buddha and asks that same question: *How hard should I be trying?* The Buddha answered, *You were a musician before you became a monk. You played the lute. Do you remember tuning your instrument? If you tuned the string too tightly, it would sound sharp and it might even snap. If you tuned to too loosely, it would flop around and make no sound. If you tuned it just so, it would come into tune. It would be in harmony with all the other strings.*

Understanding how much effort to apply when meditating is like understanding how to tune an instrument. Even if you are not a musician, you can get the analogy. How much effort you put in is unique to you. Each person experiments and finds the balance. This is the art of meditation.

The majority of people try too hard. We do this because we want to get away from discomfort. The restless mind is uncomfortable. The mind that is wanting something is uncomfortable. The mind that is hating or disliking something is uncomfortable. We would like to get rid of it, so we try to push it away. Paradoxically, the way to reduce and then eliminate such discomfort in the mind is to accept it as it is and observe thoughts and feelings as they arise and disappear. No feeling or thought stays around forever. They are all coming into being and vanishing.

Alive Exercise

How do we become aware, here and now? One way is to notice that your body is sitting here. Feel your bottom in the chair. Now, feel your back. Notice the sensations in your right hand. Take your right hand and let it move around a little bit. Move the fingers of your right hand. Then your left hand. Bring up both hands and have them come together in a silent clap and notice when they touch. When they touch, quietly say *touching*. Then, separating your hands, notice that they are no longer touching. Bring them together again, notice the touching. Separate them again, notice they are no longer touching.

When we are aware of what is happening now, we are not in the past or future. We are in the present. We are aware of being alive in the present. Any moment we are aware in the present movement, we are not lost in the wandering mind.

Concentration: A Mental Faculty

In order to train the mind to wake up and stay in the present, you do exercises to strengthen certain mental faculties, just like you lift weights to strengthen certain muscles. You don't try to lift a thousand pounds in one go and hold it up indefinitely. Instead, you lift a relatively light dumbbell many times, hold it up briefly each time, then let it back down. With meditation, you strengthen your concentration when you bring the mind back to your breath and then pay careful attention to the little details of the sensations as the breath comes and goes. The more you do this, the stronger your concentration gets.

Concentration is the mind's ability to select an object of experience and remain focused there. It counters the restless and agitated tendencies of the mind and allows awareness to perceive and penetrate into the deeper reality of the observed phenomenon. Like a microscope or a telescope, concentration sharpens the mind's focus. Many people misunderstand concentration to be the whole point of meditation. They want to suppress all other experiences, stop thinking and experience a silent and pleasant transcendental state. While this can be restful and sometimes even blissful, it is a form of escapism that is ultimately disappointing. Concentration must be balanced by mindfulness and other wholesome mental capacities.

Misuse of Concentration

Forty-five years ago I met a man who was attending his first meditation retreat. His intent was to stay for an entire month. He had been meditating for many years with a strong emphasis on concentration. Without fail, every morning and evening, he meditated. In a short time, he was able to enter into a trance state that he found very comfortable. He was quite proud of this and the fact that he had a perfect record of meditating twice daily. What he was not aware of was that he had been using concentration meditation to shut down his feelings and thoughts, and as a way to suppress awareness of situations in his life that were painful and untenable. He had become disconnected from his heart and emotions. A few days into the retreat, the feelings and thoughts that he had suppressed for years broke through. He became very agitated and confused and contemplated leaving the retreat. He complained that the meditation was making his mind worse. With great distress he realized that he was miserable in his marriage and hated his job. He had used concentration meditation to bypass his body sensations and emotions. He had been using his meditation to stay unaware of very painful parts of his life experience. After a few days, the teacher of that retreat told the fellow to go home and tend to the reality of his life. He encouraged the man to continue meditation in a less intense way than the retreat, and to incorporate awareness of his body, feelings and emotions into his practice.

The First Breath

The first formal training exercise Buddha taught was, *Become aware of your breathing.*

Breathing is a central sign of life. I was present at the birth of both of my children. When you see the child emerge from the mother and breathe in their first breath, you see how breathing is a sign of life. Everyone in the room relaxes and takes their own deep breath. All of a sudden, a new person is born. I have also been present at the time of death. The same thing happens in reverse. There is a final breathing out, and then life ends.

We breathe because we must. We are not separate from the earth. Alan Watts, one of the first to bring Eastern philosophy to the West in modern times, wrote in his book *The Book on the Taboo Against Knowing Who You Are,* "we do not 'come into this world'; we come out of it, as leaves from a tree. As the ocean 'waves' the universe 'peoples.' Every individual is an expression of the whole realm of nature, a unique action of the total universe."

We are the earth. We breathe for a lifetime and then return to earth. Most of the time we breathe without awareness that we are breathing. However, we can develop our capacity for awareness of our breath.

Breathing Exercise

Take three big deep breaths.

Can you feel the sensation in your chest or abdomen? If you can't, take a hand and place it on your chest. Do this often.

This is a training exercise. You can think of it as home base. Every time you do this exercise, you are awake in the present moment. If it gets boring or your mind wanders, then you can use little mental notes, little words in the mind. Note *rising* as you breathe in, and *falling* as you breathe out.

Fingers Touching Exercise

Touch the tips of your little fingers together, then the fourth and the third and so on, to the thumbs, softly saying *touching* each time you touch. Now take them apart from each other in the opposite order, softly saying *parting* with each parting. Do this several times. It's kind of fun. I'll bet that when you did that, there was not any worrying happening, because you were right here in the present moment.

Walking Meditations

Walking meditations are really very simple. Choose a space, about twenty to thirty feet in length. Stand at one end. Notice that you are standing and become aware of your legs. Observe how it is necessary to create an intention in the mind prior to the first step. Let the intention act and observe how the foot lifts as you take a step. Notice as it moves through the air. Notice as it reaches the ground and the feeling of the ground under the foot. When you discover your mind wandering and not attentive to the body simply return gently to the actual sensations of walking. This is similar to sitting meditation; however, instead of paying attention to the breathing, you pay attention to the actual sensations of walking in your body.

You can practice this exercise when you are running or walking from the door to your car or the bus stop, or through the airport terminal to your departure gate. It can turn the feeling of rushing into a mindfulness practice by simply becoming aware that you are moving quickly. It is a simple way to practice mindfulness while you are on the go.

Everyday Task Mindfulness Exercise

Get a package of little star stickers, the kind your teacher may have put on your homework to reward you for doing a good job. Place the little stars in odd places in your home and at work. When you notice the star, say, *Oh, right, I am here.*

For example, put a little star on the wall in your bathroom. Notice when you bathe, *Here I am stepping into the shower, right here and now, doing what I am doing.* Put one on your computer, and when you open it up or turn it on, notice, *Here I am turning on my computer*. A star by the knife rack reminds you to be mindful when you are chopping vegetables, *Now I am chopping vegetables. It's just this.* A star by the sink reminds you to note, *Now I am doing dishes; this is what I am doing now.* Put one on the front door so you see it when you leave home—awareness arises of pushing and opening the door and stepping into the outdoors.

Awareness practice does not need to be stilted, heavy or tense. It is very natural. It can be, *Now I am standing before the door. Here I am pushing the door. Here is the door opening.* When you go to your car, it can be, *Here I am pulling out my key. Here I am sitting down. Here I am, putting the car in reverse. This is what I am doing just now.*

The One-Minute-a-Day Exercise

Create a meditation area for yourself in your home. Make your place beautiful to you. Maybe it is a certain cushion on the couch or a corner of a room. You may need to try a few places around your home before you find the spot that's right for you. If you do not have a place to call home or if you travel a lot, you can create a space by wrapping yourself in a large scarf or blanket that you reserve for meditation, or by holding an object, such as a bead. Choose a wrap or object that conveys a sense of love and care to you and use it only for your meditation.

It's helpful if there is quiet and not a lot of distractions around. It is also helpful if the spot is well lit, so you do not tend to fall asleep. There is good reason to meditate in a quiet place. It aids in concentration. You may live in a noisy area or in a home with children. If you are sensitive to sound and cannot get away from noise, use ear plugs or get a good pair of headphones, the kind that completely cover the ear and are padded with foam. You may try using both the ear plugs and the headphones if you live in a loud place.

Of course, ultimately, you will learn to be mindful in the noisiest of situations and you won't need the ear protection.

Make a vow, *I am going to do this every day for one minute for the next four weeks with no exceptions.*

Pick a time in the day that is not just before bed, because if you meditate then, you will likely experience fatigue and fall asleep. Pick a time in the day when your energy is the most clear. If you are a morning person, pick a time in the morning. If you are a night owl, pick a time early in the night when your energy is highest. Get a calendar and keep it at your meditation spot. Each day you meditate, give yourself a smiley face or star on the calendar. You will encounter a day when you simply do not want to meditate. You will perhaps encounter the *I hate doing this* mind. Give yourself no slack. You vowed to practice every day, so keep your promise to yourself. Sit down for just one minute and see if you can find your breath. In this one minute, you will have the chance to come face-to-face with whatever is deflecting you from meditating. This is an essential discovery. You will be able to see what thoughts and emotions are present, and how unpleasant they are.

At the end of the four weeks, you have fulfilled your commitment. Then maybe you might decide to meditate every day for four weeks for at least five minutes, then ten or fifteen.

Try it. See what happens.

The Ten-Year-Plan Exercise

Ancient spiritual wisdom says it is best to dig one deep well rather than many shallow ones. If mindfulness practice works for you, decide that you will do it for five or ten years. Find a teacher, a community and meditating friends. Go to a retreat at least once a year. Your life will gradually transform. If you take the time to train the mind on a daily basis, bringing mindfulness into your daily life is the single most powerful thing you can do to bring happiness into your life, and to bring peace into the world.

2

Becoming More Human

The Role of Suffering in Buddhism

THE PRACTICE OF MINDFULNESS is about becoming more fully human. We become more fully human by fully engaging in life and awakening to and embracing all the pleasures and pains that arise. When we really pay attention, the pleasures and pains of life can be a vehicle for being fully human. In order to be thoroughly engaged in life, we must experience deep interpersonal attachment at some point in our lives. Being raised as a completely functioning child requires deep emotional attachment. Having intimate, fulfilling relationships also requires deep emotional attachment. But profound suffering is an inevitable consequence of these attachments because loss or the threat of loss is inescapable. Suffering arises when we cling to our attachments. When we do this, we are clinging to how we want life to be rather than the way it is. This is the price of living life fully in the world.

I do the best I can to embrace the full range of pleasure and pain that life offers. I have a family, earn a living, raise children and participate in community. In Buddhism, this is sometimes called the layperson's life. My aspiration is to live this life fully and to learn from every experience

Mindfulness practice does not mean you will not hurt anymore. It does not mean you will not have normal human reactions or that you will transcend your feelings. It does mean you will start to experience all your feelings more intensely because you are paying attention.

By allowing ourselves to be open with loving awareness to all the experiences of life, we come into a different and empowered relationship with them. We learn to ride the waves of pleasure/pain, gain/loss and sickness/

health with equanimity and compassion. When we don't react unconsciously to suffering, we begin to have a choice in how we respond to it, and
our lives become more manageable.

Our lives radically change when we mindfully observe suffering in the
mind or body. When we observe it, we can choose not to identify with it.
When we stop identifying with it, we stop reflexively reacting and making
things in our life worse. By resting in awareness, we can make behavioral
changes and become more kind and caring.

Where Does Suffering Come From?

"Dahlink, there is always a leak in the canoe." With these colorful words,
my teacher Ruth Denison expressed the Buddha's First Noble Truth. One
way to understand the First Noble Truth is: despite our best efforts to create
lives that are stable, comfortable, loving and happy, the common experience for all of us is that life is hard and utterly unpredictable.

Suffering is obvious when we are living in a war zone or trapped in
poverty. In these situations, people are constantly engaged in a struggle to
survive, often lacking food, shelter, basic safety, medical care and much
more. But suffering is also a reality when we have all the apparent security
modern life can offer. Even the most wealthy and powerful of us suffer.
Everybody, no matter how rich or poor, faces disappointment, separation,
sickness, old age and death.

Suffering is inevitable because life is unstable. Everything is constantly
changing. Even the best of situations change and will end. We are healthy,
then we get sick. Relationships come and go. The stock market zooms to
new heights then crashes. We age, and our beauty and physical strength
fade. We invest tremendous energy into plans that fail to come true.

Compounding all that is the fact that we go to great lengths to avoid
encountering the reality of suffering. We intoxicate ourselves with alcohol
or drugs. We go shopping. We plan an exciting vacation. We overeat. We
overwork.

Buddha taught that in our journey through life we inevitably encounter suffering through the experiences of birth, sickness, old age, decay and
death. He articulated four other categories of experience that lead to disappointment and suffering.

These are:

- Having experiences you do not want to have.
- Not having experiences you do want to have.
- Being with someone you do not want to be with.
- Not being with someone you do want to be with.

Please take a few moments to reflect. Does this list resonate with you? Do you recognize any of these experiences? Are they not part of the fabric of your everyday life? Do you struggle to create a world in which these inevitable circumstances are not present?

If this list resonates with you, you are in good company, as these experiences represent the human condition.

While we work desperately to make the outer world stable through quests for money, success, celebrity or social status, we strive even more diligently to make our minds stable. Despite our best efforts, we encounter storms of anxiety, depression, hatred, self-hatred, remorse, loneliness, jealousy and more.

Our moods color our every experience and are constantly changing. We want pleasant moods to persist and unpleasant moods to vanish, never arise again, yet we wield little influence or control over any of them.

Have you discovered a nagging or debilitating dissatisfaction that accompanies you through life? Perhaps that is why you are reading this book. It was this realization that sent the young Siddhartha Gotama, later known as Buddha, on his spiritual quest. His term for this dissatisfaction was *dukkha*, which is commonly translated as suffering. Dukkha is also translated as difficult to bear, unpleasantness, stress, and the mind struggling against things as they are. The origin of the word *dukkha* comes from the grinding that occurs when there is grit caught in a wheel bearing.

Dukkha is the First Noble Truth of Buddha. People hear this and sometimes say that Buddhism is a dismal downer, but it can be a great relief to realize our experience of suffering is normal and is, in fact, the doorway to happiness. Recognizing the truth of dukkha is similar to getting a clear diagnosis for an illness: the cause is known and, as you will see, there is a treatment that cures.

Buddha Was Not a Buddhist

Buddha lived in what is now Nepal and North India about 2,600 years ago. He was an ordinary human being who discovered the path to awakening. He taught for more than forty years and developed the teachings that we follow today. He was able to guide others to have the same experience of freedom and personal transformation that he did.

If you choose to follow this path, as countless people have done before, you too can find freedom.

The collection of stories, texts and practices that come down to us from that time are known as Buddhism, but it's important to note that Buddha was not a Buddhist. He didn't teach much of what has come to be known as Buddhism, and he would not recognize much of what is called Buddhism today. He taught the Dharma, a way of life and practice that enhances the capacity of human beings to live in harmony with each other, and a way of training the heart and mind that leads individuals to greater happiness and freedom, including the ultimate freedom of awakening.

When I first encountered Buddhism, almost fifty years ago, I had been struggling to free myself from a dogmatic and rigid childhood religious training. I had traded the Catholic church for the church of the outdoors and nature. I spent much of my life skiing and mountain climbing. From my training in college, I was deeply embedded in the scientific method and unwilling to blindly swallow a set of religious beliefs. On my first Buddhist meditation retreat, I was comforted by a traditional story in which Buddha warned people about blind belief. It is known as Buddha's teachings to the Kalamas.

After his awakening, Buddha wandered and taught throughout northern India. When he spoke to the Kalama clan in their city of Kesaputta, they were very skeptical. These people, known as the Kalamas, had heard many wandering teachers claiming their teachings were the only truth while disparaging other outlooks.

The Kalamas asked Buddha, *Why should we believe you?*

He responded, *By all means don't.*

This is a refreshing response from a spiritual teacher, don't you think?

Buddha said, *Don't believe me blindly, but also don't throw the baby out with the bathwater. Test what I teach and see if it really works. You can see if it works in this way: Does what I teach lead to a discernible reduction in suffering for yourself? Does it lead to a reduction in greed, hatred and ignorance? Does it lead to less suffering for your loved ones? And does it result in all beings suffering less? If you test the teachings in this way, you will know if they really work. You will have them as an experience, not just as a set of beliefs. If this is not your experience, if it does not work for you, then do not follow them.*

This teaching to the Kalamas, and to us, endows us with tremendous responsibility. It is up to each individual to determine if the practice really works.

I encourage you to test it for yourself. After reading this book, practice Buddha's teachings on mindfulness for one month. At the end of one month, ask yourself the following: Does it work? Am I happier? Is there less anxiety in my life? Do I experience more ease? Am I able to accept life's difficulties with more grace?

The Map Is Not the Territory

When we look at a map, it is clear that the map is not the territory itself. A map is a symbolic representation of hills, valleys, forests, rivers, mountains and roads. Similarly, the Dharma teachings are a highly articulated map of life and consciousness. While Dharma is the word that is used to describe Buddha's teachings, it also means *the truth of the way things actually are.* Dharma is not a religion. It is not intended to be taken on blind faith.

One could take the Dharma as divinely inspired truth and hold the teachings as a dogma. This could lead to blind belief and a lack of willingness to question and explore for oneself whether the map is an accurate representation of the landscape of one's inner experience.

Buddha said that the only thing we can rely on is our direct experience. If the Dharma works for you, then it serves as a map that makes the journey of life more meaningful and the path safer. It helps you avoid pitfalls and trips down blind valleys with no exit.

Let me propose a theory: that feelings of greed, aversion and hatred and their companion feelings (frustration, boredom, irritation, confusion, etc.) are in themselves suffering, and that experiences of suffering can be stepping stones on a path to enlightenment. If we accept this theory, then we can try the Kalama experiment for ourselves.

For the next month, carry out this experiment. Ask yourself these three questions each day:

- Is it true it is painful when my mind is colored with greed, aversion or hatred?

- Is it true that suffering follows when I act from greed, aversion or hatred?

- What happens when I don't act upon my feelings of greed, aversion or hatred?

Use a journal to take notes as you carry out this experiment. Record how you acted when feelings of greed, aversion and hatred came up. When you've done the hard work of asking these questions and mindfully observed your responses, then you can decide for yourself whether the teachings are worth following. At the same time, you've also taught yourself how to live—a learning that can bring joy and the energy to go even deeper.

This is a practice that bears fruit quickly and continues to bear the fruit of a greater capacity to accept life on its own terms, and therefore to be more loving. It is a practice we can do for the rest of our lives.

Noticing the Urge to Move: Bearing the Seemingly Unbearable in Small Doses

Have you ever noticed how we are constantly changing our position physically? We have an itch and scratch it. We stretch our neck. We shift our posture.

If you go to the symphony, watch how everyone sits very still and then, right after the last cadenza when the piece ends, most audience members adjust their bodies, clear their throats, and generally respond to all the pent-up demand to move.

Why are we moving so much? Because the human body is constantly in discomfort or pain. From the moment we are born, there is something aching, something itching, something we are trying to fix.

Not surprisingly, such restlessness manifests itself when we come to meditation. We might say, *For the next twenty minutes, I am going to just sit here.* Quite quickly, though, something unpleasant inevitably comes up. We say to ourselves, *I don't like that.* As mammals, as living beings, when something hurts or feels uncomfortable, we move to avoid the pain or discomfort. This makes sense. Our survival as a species requires that we avoid pain. If I put my finger in a burning candle, it would not take very long for my body to send the signal, *Ouch! Move that finger!* Those beings that did not receive and heed the signal of pain would suffer injury, infection and other complications, and did not get to pass on their DNA.

This is not a practice of denying the useful requests of the body. Rather, it is simply a practice of understanding just how unconsciously reactive we are. Have you ever scratched your face without noticing, or seen someone else do this? Perhaps you noticed after the fact and realized you were completely unaware when you were scratching.

Let's say you are sitting in meditation and an itchy feeling in the face arises. You notice it and come back to the breath. You notice it again. You come back to the breath again. You do not move. If the discomfort continues to call your attention, you may choose to mindfully put down the attention to breathing and mindfully turn awareness to the itching. You investigate it. You observe how the resistance to it is the cause of suffering.

Why would you do this? You are learning to bear the seemingly unbearable in very small doses. You give yourself a choice in how you respond to situations. You no longer are compelled to react on the basis of instinct or entrenched coping mechanisms.

With this exercise, you become more awake: the capacity to bear the unbearable physically helps you learn how to bear the unbearable emotionally.

Eventually, over time, we find we can sit in meditation and observe moods as they swing from high and happy to low and unpleasant and then high again. We also learn how to be with physical discomfort, which is essential, because in our lives there will surely be times of physical pain. We will all experience sickness, old age, decay and death.

If you want to become more kind and loving, it behooves you to learn how to suffer discomfort and pain consciously and with an open heart. If you do not learn how to bear discomfort, when times get tough you wind up lashing out and hurting your loved ones. Sitting still with the small itches and aches is a strategy for learning how to be with the great pains of life.

In order to transform our lives our practice must extend far beyond the meditation cushion. We learn to pay attention to how we are dealing with the range of suffering we encounter in all aspects of life, from small discomforts to major events. We discover that all of our compulsions and addictions are coping strategies for discomfort. It is difficult to maintain awareness when suffering. When we are suffering, it is particularly difficult to discover the real cause of our suffering. We have very strong tendencies to alter consciousness with alcohol, drugs or other diversions like television, smartphones, social media, shopping or work, rather than face the challenge of waking up. Some of our coping mechanisms are not inherently bad activities, but when you are overworking, intoxicated, binge watching a show or spending hours on your latest favorite app, you are typically in a trance. You are simply not present to your own life, and you are unaware of what is happening inside you or outside.

Mindfulness is the practice of being in the present and awake to the flow of pleasant and unpleasant experiences that are arising and passing away in the body and mind with love, compassion and wisdom for ourselves and all that is. With mindfulness we learn that all states are transient and that we don't have to constantly react in a habitual fashion. We practice every day to strengthen our capacity to find relief from suffering by sitting with the discomfort and learning to bear the unbearable.

Unpleasant Experiences Exercise

This exercise may seem odd at first. You should never do this exercise in a way or at a time when you would cause yourself real harm. The first time you do this exercise, set your timer for thirty seconds. Close your eyes and bring to mind something from your past that causes you sorrow, anger or pain. It may be something minor, like being overcharged for an item you bought, or it may be a major life event. Allow the memory to come into the mind as fully as it can. At the thirty-second ringer, reset the timer for another thirty seconds. Notice how your body feels. Notice the proliferation of thoughts, feelings and impulses. Notice the judgments that come up about these. When the second thirty-second timer goes off, congratulate yourself for doing the exercise. As you develop your muscle for this exercise, you will gradually develop an ability to notice when the thoughts, feelings, and impulses are arising without the timer.

3

Life of Buddha

AT THE HEART OF every culture there is a myth that helps people organize and bring meaning to their lives. Myths provide invaluable maps of our inner lives.

The Buddha was an actual person who lived in northern India. He lived for eighty-one years and his example and teaching, which have religious, spiritual and mythic importance, have had a lasting effect upon the world. As is always the case, the stories of his life and teachings have been embellished. The story of Buddha has mythological aspects to it, as does any story passed down for centuries. In this chapter, I make direct connections between some of the mythological attributes of Buddha's story and the dilemmas all of us face in the reality of our lives today.

As you read, please listen for the detail that touches you, or is particularly alive for you. Remember that this story takes place in the realm of mythology, where truths are told through metaphor and image.

The Great Illusion

Once upon a time, there was a small kingdom called Kapilavastu located on the border between what we now call India and Nepal. Kapilavastu was a small kingdom between two very large and powerful states called Magadha and Kosila. The king was Suddhodana and the queen was Mahamaya which means *Great Illusion*.

It was a feudal society, in which succession occurred by blood from father to son. Despite their best efforts, Queen Mahamaya failed to conceive, posing a grave danger to the kingdom. Month after month with no baby.

Imagine adding to that suffering the lack of an heir to the throne—ending their line of succession.

Following the customs of her time, Queen Mahamaya planned to go north into the mountains, to a place where women had gone forever to perform the fertility rites and rituals to have a baby. She left Kapilavastu riding in her palanquin carried on poles on the shoulders of her servants.

They went north for several days, up into the mountains of eternal snow, the Himalayas, to a sacred place of fertility known only to the women. Once there, she bathed, was anointed with the finest oils and scents and carried out all the necessary rituals. She lay in a comfortable and elegant bed and fell into a deep sleep. It was a dreamless sleep, until the darkest moment of the night, when she had a vivid dream.

She dreamt that coming from the east was a great white tusker elephant that entered her through her left side. She woke with a start, as tends to happen with such dreams. She told her maidservants, *It has happened. We can return to Kapilavastu now. All will be well.*

You can imagine the excitement in Kapilavastu when she returned and the dream was made known. King Suddhodana called his seers—his astrologers, soothsayers and wise men. The seers looked at the stars and they looked at tea leaves. They looked at the entrails of chickens. Something was wrong. They did not come out from their deliberations smiling. Instead, they emerged with long faces.

King Suddhodana could sense this immediately. He said, *What is the problem?* They were reluctant to say what they saw. The chief seer said, *The portent is mixed. You will have a son, but it is unclear whether he will become a great world ruler and rule all the known world, or whether he will renounce the worldly life and become a world teacher.*

King Suddhodana was distraught. He needed a son who would take over the kingdom; otherwise the neighboring kingdoms would gobble it up. There would be in-fighting. There would be destruction. There would be death.

King Suddhodana and his councilors created a plan. They decided they would protect this child from all forms of suffering. They would build special palaces for different seasons. Thus, they thought, he would be protected from all suffering and live in such luxury that he would have no interest in spiritual questioning.

He would never scrape his knee.

He would never have a pet die.

He would never have a bad mood.

He would have none of the childhood illnesses.

He would know only pleasure.

The king determined that he would protect his son from all the disappointments and painful experiences of life, so that his son would grow up without any knowledge that suffering exists.

Powerful Like a River

After the seers had shared their ominous news, and King Suddhodana had decided to shield the child from all suffering, there appeared at the palace door one of the most well-known and elderly mystics of the time, a renowned seeker. His name was Ashita, which means "powerful like a river." This was a time when "seeking"—seeking awakening—was very well respected. The seeker came in, and when he heard what was happening, began to sob and wail. Imagine, a highly respected seeker and long-term meditator in his elder years sobbing and wailing. Ashita said, *I am crushed. I know that this birth is going to produce a Buddha, an awakened one. And I will die before I hear his teachings.*

Heavens Above and Worlds Below, There's No One Quite Like Me

Months passed. Queen Mahamaya cleaned up her diet, avoided alcohol, took her vitamins, got lots of sleep, meditated, and practiced yoga to prepare her body for birth. Finally, the time came for the birth of her child. As was the custom in those days, she prepared to go to her family in the neighboring kingdom to have her baby. She set off once again in her palanquin, and labor began on the journey. Her servants helped her out of the palanquin, and she walked into the forest by herself. She gave birth standing up, holding the branch of a sala tree. The baby was born feet first. When he hit the ground, he took ten steps and cried out, *Heavens above and worlds below, there is no one quite like me.*

This, of course, is the cry of every baby. Each of us is a unique, one of a kind being in the universe.

The Loss of the Great Illusion

With her newborn baby bundled in her arms, Queen Mahamaya returned to her palanquin and headed back toward Kapilavastu. Here, the story takes a dark turn. As has happened to so many millions of women, giving birth caused her death.

Queen Mahamaya, the Great Illusion, died.

The new prince needed to be mothered. And so the job fell to Queen Mahapajapati Gotami, the sister of Queen Mahamaya, who was also a wife of King Suddhodana. As was the custom in those days, he had married both of them at the same time. Mahapajapati Gotami means *Great Leader of the Assembly.*

The death of the child's mother provokes an interesting contemplation from a psycho-historical point of view. This death was an early family-of-origin wound. A little baby lost his mother. A little baby was the cause of his mother's death. Might that have helped set the stage for his quest to relieve suffering? Was this his original wound, which occurred even before the King could start to protect him from suffering?

It usually takes suffering to bring people to meditation and a spiritual quest. Are there traumas or losses in your own life that contribute to your quest?

The Lap of Luxury

The boy was named Siddhartha, reflecting the predictions that he was *Destined for Greatness.* His aunt, Queen Mahapajapati Gotami had become his stepmother. Of course, he had nurses who took care of him. He lived in the lap of luxury. His father, stepmother and nurses did everything they possibly could to keep him safe, protected, healthy and happy. When it was too hot in Kapilavastu, they went to a palace in the mountains that had been built for him. He always had the finest entertainments and distractions: the most succulent fruits, delicious meals, graceful dancers, sweetest music, entertaining theater.

There was intrigue and conflict between kingdoms, so it was essential to the safety of the kingdom that a great king come into being. As the boy grew up, he was given the finest education. He debated with his teachers the same philosophical questions that we debate today. He was trained to be a diplomat and king. Because he was from the warrior caste, he was trained in martial arts. He developed all the competencies to be a great king who could lead his army into battle and protect the kingdom.

The Fetter

The time came for Prince Siddhartha to marry. There was a very beautiful young woman in a nearby kingdom named Yasodhara, which means *Companion to Greatness*. As was the custom, in order to seek her hand one had to prevail in a martial arts competition. Everyone knew that she would be a special bride, so young men came from far and wide to demonstrate their skill. We don't know what Yasodhara thought or felt, but we can imagine that it could be overwhelming, perhaps even frightening, to have all these men come to do battle for her hand in marriage. However, there was one young man who, when he appeared, she knew immediately would be the winner. She felt profoundly drawn to him. This suitor was, of course, Siddhartha. On the day of the competition, this one young man outshone the rest.

There was a great royal wedding with feasting, music, dancing, acrobats and celebration. King Suddhodana took a great breath of relief as he saw the young Siddhartha follow the prescribed, conventional path toward his throne. Once Siddhartha had a wife, and then a family, he would certainly not abandon worldly life!

After some time, Siddhartha and Yasodhara had a son. They named him Rahula which, interestingly, means *Fetter*. (A fetter is a device, usually one of a pair of rings connected to a chain, that is attached to the ankles or feet to restrict movement.)

Sickness

Indian religion and myth at the time of the Buddha were similar to that of the Greeks. Just as the Greek gods were described as looking down on the world of humans from heaven and occasionally intervening, so did the Brahmans of Hindu mythology. As they watched the unfolding story of Siddhartha, what they saw disturbed them. They said, *We've been waiting for a fully awakened being. We've been waiting eons for a Buddha. We sent that one, but it looks like he's going to be a political leader instead.* One of them suggested, *Well, why don't we just shake things up a little bit?*

So, they sent three heavenly messengers, and one earthly one. We might think of this as sending angels to the realm of humans.

One day Siddhartha was out riding in his chariot with Channa, his charioteer and martial arts master. In keeping with the wishes of King Sudhodhana, the city had been specially cleaned up everywhere they rode. No riffraff were to be seen. Security was tight. The buildings were painted and the townsfolk were all dressed up.

As Siddhartha came riding into town in his chariot, Channa standing right beside him, Siddhartha saw something unusual.

There was a man lying by the side of the road.

It was the first heavenly messenger.

Siddhartha told Channa to stop. Channa, remembering the instructions of the king, did not want to.

Siddhartha insisted. *Stop!*

Siddhartha got down from the chariot. He approached the man, who was deathly ill, something he'd never seen before. Siddhartha had never had a childhood disease, not even a cold or a sniffle.

Gaping at this very sick man, he asked, *Channa, what is that?*

Channa said, *Well, that is called sickness.*

Siddhartha's brain was reeling. He said, *Sickness! Could that happen to you, Channa?*

Yes.

Could that happen to me?

Yes.

Could that happen to Yasodhara?

Yes.

Could this sickness happen to my son, Rahula?

Yes, it could.

The mood in the chariot on the way back to the castle was subdued, and in some versions, it is said that Siddhartha became moody, depressed and withdrawn. He wasn't so interested in the dancing girls, competing with his fighting buddies and holding philosophical discussions. The shine and shimmer of ordinary life and the consolation prizes of pleasure and achievement had begun to tarnish.

Old Age

The Hindu gods were not done confronting Siddhartha's ignorance. They sent a second heavenly messenger. This time in the form of a very old person.

Again, Siddhartha and Channa are riding along. Siddhartha spots an old, frail person and tells Channa to stop. Again, Channa does not want to stop, and again Siddhartha insists. Siddhartha gets down from the chariot, approaches the elderly person and is appalled.

Siddhartha asks Channa, *What is this?*

Channa says, *Well, this is called old age.*

Could this happen to you?

Well, yes. In fact, this will happen to me.

Could this happen to me?.

Yes, it could. It will.

Could this happen to Yasodhara?

At this point, Siddhartha imagines his beautiful young wife becoming old and frail.

Could this happen to my son, Rahula?

Yes, my prince. This is the destiny of all living creatures.

Once again, the mood in the chariot on the way home was rather dark.

This section of the story may remind you of similar events in your own life. Have you been to a nursing home or spent time with an elderly person who can't speak anymore? These are painful and enlightening circumstances to witness. I visited my mother in a nursing home in British Columbia for the last six years of her life. Although I sometimes left at lunchtime because I found it too painful to be there, occasionally I stayed. I got down off my chariot and let my heart open. One time, a nurse asked if I would help feed some of the women in the nursing home. There was one very old woman who had skin like parchment paper. She was almost a skeleton. The only way she would eat was if a spoon of food touched her lip. She opened her mouth. I put in a spoonful of food. Then her mouth closed and she swallowed. That's how she stayed alive. While I was feeding this woman, the nurse came by and asked, *Do you have any idea who you are feeding?*

I answered, *No.*

She said, *This was Canada's prima ballerina in the '20s. She was the greatest dancer in the world. She traveled all over the world and danced for huge audiences.*

This reality was shocking for me. This ancient, frail woman had not always been like this. Only a few years ago she was a vibrant and beautiful dancer with a complex life and great fame.

In my mother's case, a stroke paralyzed her left side, leading to a dislocated shoulder. She lived in constant pain for six years until her death. She also had lost control of her emotions. She could speak fairly well, but there were a lot of gaps in cognition. Whenever I entered the room, she started to sob like a baby . . . *waaahhh*. Crying, crying, crying.

Then she would blurt out, *Tell me to stop, tell me to stop*.

I loudly responded, *Stop, Eleanor!* And she stopped.

Visiting her over all those years, ever so slowly, chipped away at my denial.

As one of the teachings of the Buddha says, *I am of the nature to age I have not gone beyond aging.*

Death

While Siddhartha was again riding in the chariot with Channa, a third heavenly messenger arrived, in the form of a corpse . . . Death.

Stop the chariot.

Siddhartha got down.

What is this?!!

On the ground before him was a lifeless corpse, somewhat disfigured.

Oh. This is death, said Channa.

Siddhartha asked the same questions as before; the same answers were given. Siddhartha was even more distressed that before.

Now think about your own experiences with the heavenly messengers. Do you recognize yourself in this story? Did you ever think, *I'm not supposed to get sick and die!* Do you remember when your illusion that you would never fall ill was shattered? Until then, you probably thought you'd live forever. But maybe a loved one became very ill, or a parent died, or a neighbor's child was diagnosed with cancer.

I have observed many times over my years of teaching that people come to the Dharma for a period then retreat. They come into close orbit for a while, practicing regularly on their own, listening to Dharma talks and attending meditation sessions. Sometimes they go to a retreat or two. Then life gets really good, overt suffering diminishes, and they stop practicing. Sometimes years later, sometimes sooner, something happens to shatter the illusion that everything is going to stay pleasant forever. They experience a failure, a close death, illness, heartache, or some other form of suffering. They remember that there is a path that leads to freedom from suffering and once again are motivated to practice.

Many people come to mindfulness practice when they have met the heavenly messengers.

The Great Going Forth

The Hindu gods sent a fourth messenger, this time a wandering ascetic, a seeker. This wandering monk, wearing rags, carrying a staff and a begging bowl, had a very calm countenance. His face was serene and open.

The seeker wanders into Siddhartha's path. Siddhartha sees him. Siddhartha asks Channa, *What's that?*

Channa replies, *That is a wandering ascetic, one who has renounced the world. He has gone forth and is seeking freedom from suffering.*

Siddhartha then realizes that he isn't the only one who is disenchanted with worldly life. He finds this thought to be very disruptive. Thoughts of how upset his father would be if he renounced his kingship kept churning in his mind. There was something inside him that simply would not rest.

This all came to a head one particular evening. It was to be Siddhartha's last evening in the kingdom. He was watching yet another show of beautiful dancers and musicians. He watched as young men and women performed amazing acrobatic feats. Their costumes and makeup were perfect. Their performances were perfect. Their voices were perfect. All these entertainments were . . . wonderful. Perfectly . . . distracting. That night, the heir to the throne couldn't sleep.

Late into the night, as he wandered about the castle, Siddhartha came upon the room where the evening's performers slept. They were snoring. Their clothes were put aside . . . and they smelled bad. He saw that they'd had to work hard that evening. What he saw confirmed what he had seen with Channa those days before: the shadow side of things, the reality behind the curtains. He decided, *I will go forth! I will not become the King.*

Siddhartha couldn't leave without saying goodbye to his wife and child. He went to their bedroom and looked in. He realized, *If I go into that room, I will never be able to leave.* And so he turned away.

Have you ever had a moment when you realized that your life was taking a radically different course? Have you felt plans you'd made suddenly turn to dust? Do you remember the sense of confusion, loss and uncertainty as something bubbled up from within that you could no longer avoid?

Siddhartha told Channa to saddle his great white war horse, Kanthaka, his companion since youth, and meet him with Kanthaka at the postern gate. Siddhartha took one last look back, and they rode off into the night. Siddhartha and Channa rode for many hours through the night until they came to a place that seemed far enough away.

Siddhartha got down off Kanthaka and took his sword in his hand for the last time. He reached behind his head and grabbed his long hair, which had never been cut. He cut it off as close to his head as he could. At that moment, Kanthaka, his great war horse, dropped dead. Siddhartha gave the hair to Channa and said, *Be my messenger and don't fail me. Take this hair to my father and tell him, "Do not follow Siddhartha." Tell him I will not come back.*

Imagine what a challenging decision this was for Siddhartha. Intuition was telling him that his destiny required him to leave, but his rational mind was listing all the reasons why he should stay—his father, stepmother, wife and child. The tension between these opposites was excruciating.

This moment, this experience, is called *the Great Going Forth*.

It is when we realize that our old life is falling away. We can no longer be satisfied with seeking pleasure and security—and avoiding pain—through distractions. Seeking happiness through the sense doors or perceptual gateways of the mouth, eyes, ears, nose, body or mind doesn't cut it. Eating another éclair, having another drink, going on another exciting vacation, falling in love, or engaging in another hot political or philosophical discussion is increasingly unsatisfying. We find ourselves having to do something else. Our personal going forth doesn't mean that we have to leave our duties of family or work. It's most often an inner shift in which our values change and we find ourselves drawn strongly toward inner life and spiritual practice.

Now let's continue with Siddhartha's story. He was on his quest. He was on the road, on foot. He walked alone until he met a homeless person. He said to this homeless person, *I'd like to trade clothes with you.* The homeless person, seeing his clothes were of great value, traded immediately. Siddhartha was then dressed in rags.

In India at this time seeking awakening was respected. Siddhartha equipped himself with a bowl and a staff. He went forth as a sadhu, a holy person. To this day, in India sadhus are respected and supported by the community at large. Siddhartha went to the forest. He had heard there were wise teachers there.

It was the first time in northern India that there was extra food. Agriculture had been developed so survival was no longer dependent upon hunting and gathering. Enough of the jungles had been cleared that humans could experience safety from wild animals and predation when in the forest. This meant that some people could devote themselves full time to the inner life.

Siddhartha's Three Teachers

Siddhartha embarked on his path and encountered three teachers who he eventually left to pursue his own vision. Each teacher focused on one of the states known in Buddhism as the formless jhanas: infinite consciousness, no-thingness and the non-describable.

Infinite Consciousness

Siddhartha's first teacher, a man by the name of Alara Kalama, was known to be very wise. He was a master of the state of infinite consciousness.

Following the instructions of Alara Kalama, Siddhartha went into the forest to practice alone. He was very diligent in his meditation practice and quickly mastered the state of infinite consciousness. He returned to Alara Kalama and said, *I am now able to freely access infinite consciousness, what is next?*

Alara Kalama said, *This is all there is to know. Stay with me and teach. Be my co-teacher.*

Siddhartha said, *But there remains the truth of suffering: birth, sickness, old age and death. This state of infinite consciousness is temporary, and ceases when I stop concentrating and withdrawing from the world.*

Alara Kalama said, *You are misguided. This is the ultimate teaching. There is nothing more to know.*

Imagine how difficult it must have been for Siddhartha to realize that this highly respected teacher with hundreds of followers did not have the answer he was looking for. It required great integrity for Siddhartha to leave. His quest required him again and again to leave the security of the known and face the unknown.

It is the same for each of us. We face a similar dilemma when we trust our own experience and leave old secure ways behind to venture on a new path.

Siddhartha thanked Alara Kalama, respectfully bowed to him, and left.

No-Thingness

Siddhartha found a second teacher. His name was Udakka Ramaputta. He was a master of the realm of no-thingness. The same thing happened. Siddhartha quickly mastered the teaching of Udakka Ramaputta, who also invited Siddhartha to teach with him and help lead his great following.

Again, the questions about sickness, decay, old age and death arose. Siddhartha once again discovered that he had to move on.

The Non-Describable: The Realm of Neither Perception nor Non-Perception

Siddhartha found a third teacher in the forest and there he became a master of the realm of neither perception nor non-perception.

Once again, he was invited by the teacher to stay and teach with him. Once again, the reality of suffering emerged, and he went on.

Siddhartha was on his quest. He had discovered that what is now called the jhanas did not provide lasting satisfaction. The penthouse in the high rise, the private jet, the best of everything didn't result in lasting satisfaction. Infinite consciousness did not result in lasting satisfaction. Neither did no-thingness nor the non-describable.

Siddhartha had fully experienced the satisfaction of his sense desires. He had experienced the most exquisite sensual pleasure. Now he had experienced exalted states of the jhanas, the mental pleasures. Still, he was not free from suffering.

Asceticism

In fifth century BCE India there were people who believed that self-mortification could free one from suffering. These ascetics subscribed to the belief that if you never allowed the body any pleasure, you would become detached from it.

When sexual desire arises, you never partake.

When the desire for food arises, you rarely partake.

After leaving his third teacher, Siddhartha practiced asceticism. He became a one-grain-of-rice-a-day man. Of course, today this sounds very extreme to us. Many people are on very specific diets, but Siddhartha practiced all of them at the same time: low fat, low carbohydrate, gluten-free, dairy-free and vegan.

He became so emaciated that he could reach through his stomach and touch his spine. He slept out of doors, on the ground, without a mat.

He thwarted all impulses to satisfy the body's desires.

To this day, in India you can find Yogis who sleep on pointed objects, who never cut their hair, and who fast to extremes. They believe the following: *If I starve the sense doors enough, I will become free.*

Siddhartha had an intense exploratory urge. He was an ascetic for several years. He had to know directly for himself if something worked and so he practiced it to its depths.

The Milk of Human Kindness

One day Siddhartha went into the river Niranjana, which runs through Bodhgaya, during the monsoon. He went into the water and found he didn't have the strength to get out. He could feel his body losing its ability to fight the current. He was exhausted and about to give up, but just at that point he managed to claw his way up on the riverbank. He lay there, gasping, almost dead.

A young woman named Sujata saw him. She was a devotee of Brahman. She was carrying a bowl of very special milk rice, a kind of rice pudding, with the intention of offering it at the temple. The myth tells us that the milk of one hundred cows was fed to three cows. The milk of those three had been fed to one cow. The milk of that final cow had been distilled down to what we might call the milk of human kindness, and then used to cook the rice. We might also call it the divine feminine. Whatever we call it, Sujata fed it to Siddhartha. Then she nursed him back to health.

Before his near drowning, he had practiced with five other ascetics. When they saw him eating and being taken care of like this, they scorned him. They said, *Look at Siddhartha. He has fallen back into the worldly life. He's not someone to follow anymore.* The ascetics left him. Sujata and her father took care of Siddhartha until he was healthy again.

Have you ever had the experience of almost drowning, or coming close to death, or feeling like you are drowning in the circumstances of your life? How did you make use of it? Did it change you?

The Vision

During the time Siddhartha was being nursed back to health, he reflected on all his experiences. By now he was in his late twenties. As he reflected, a poignant childhood memory came to him.

Siddhartha remembered being a child at the springtime ritual of his father, the king, plowing the first furrow in the fields with a water buffalo. He remembered seeing worms being turned out of the ground by the blade, and the birds swooping in to eat them. He was confused, disgusted and saddened upon seeing the naked truth of the death of the struggling worms. He had glimpsed the violence of the natural world. His ignorance was being pierced. He turned away from the worms' misery. He found solace in a grove of sala trees. He was not aware at the time that this was his first attempt at going forth.

Sala trees produce huge, incredibly complex blooms overnight. The blooms come right out of the trunk. The perfume of the flowers carries to a great distance.

Sala trees play a significant role in this story because Siddhartha was born under a sala tree and died under one.

Have you ever gone through a big change in your life, and only noticed when you looked back that the karmic seeds of your path had been sown long before?

A vision of Siddhartha's child-self sitting under the sala tree came to him. He remembered that his mind had turned inward, in response to the violent scene he had witnessed of the birds swooping down to eat the worms. He had relinquished his tight grip on the outer world. His mind had dropped into a place of remarkable ease and relaxation, and his consciousness had been luminous.

When you look back on your childhood, do you remember having this experience? Children often do, and you probably did. This state is effortless. Any thoughts or emotions that arise don't trigger a reaction. There is contentment, and no desire to change anything. Thoughts and emotions are not a problem. There is a great deal of equanimity.

It occurred to Siddhartha that maybe this was the way to the freedom he was seeking. He had failed to find freedom by indulging all his worldly desires. Its opposite, asceticism and starvation, had also failed. Concentration alone had not set him free either. His intuition began to weave all his training, experience and lessons together. A new approach to meditation was emerging in him.

He went back to the river Niranjana, much stronger in body and mind.

Siddhartha said, *If tonight is to be the night of my awakening, I will put my bowl in the river, and it will move upstream.*

It did. It went against the stream. This is what everyone who meditates is doing: going against the stream.

He went to the foot of a great tree. It was the Bodhi tree, or the Tree of Awakening. Because of his awakening under this tree, its scientific name is ficus religiosa, the religious fig tree. Today in the village of Bodh Gaya in Bihar, India, there is a descendant of this great tree.

Siddhartha sat down under the tree and made a vow. *I am going to sit here until I awaken.*

He sat, prepared for anything.

Mara

Mara—the personification of temptation and indulgence, greed, hatred and delusion—appeared to Siddhartha as he sat under the tree.

Mara said, *Hello Siddhartha. What do you think you're doing?*

Siddhartha replied, *I have come to awaken. I have been on my quest for a long time and tonight is the night of my awakening.*

Mara said, *We'll see about that!*

Mara's Daughters

With the snap of Mara's fingers, the three most beautiful, sensuous and desirable women that ever walked the face of the earth appeared in front of Siddhartha. They were Mara's daughters.

Remember this is mythology, a map of the inner life, and not a literal rendering of facts. Siddhartha's story is the story of every human life. If Siddhartha had been of a different sexual orientation, those bodies he desired would have appeared. Or perhaps he would have been tempted by the finest chocolate, newest iPhone, a glass of fine wine, or plans for a tropical vacation. In short, your most potent desire will appear to you as you move toward awakening, and this desire will do its best to pull you off your meditation cushion.

Siddhartha was faced with the extraordinary apparition of these women. Remember, these weren't mere pictures. They were very attractive and very alive and possessed the very essence of temptation and desire.

His response to them was remarkable.

He did not say, *You're disgusting. You are corrupt and corrupting. I won't let you pull me back into the world.*

He also did not say, *I'll go with you. I can always come back here. There will be another time!*

Instead, he said, *Dear sisters, you are extraordinarily beautiful. I know that to be with you would be a potent experience of pleasure. But I have done that, and it is impermanent. It would be wonderful, and then it would be over, and I would be here again, unawakened.*

Mara's daughters vanished.

As you travel your own path, you will encounter Mara and his daughters many times in many forms. The lesson is not to eradicate desire, but instead to come to a different relationship with it, so that you neither attach to it nor reject it, but instead see it for what it is.

Anger and Fear

Mara summoned a second challenge. Armies of fear, rage, sadness, despair, loneliness, jealousy, hopelessness, self-hatred and depression appeared. They attacked. They came in close. They fired their arrows and screamed like banshees.

Siddhartha had encountered these demons so many times in his meditation that he no longer feared them. He faced them with equanimity, love and compassion. He understood love to mean that there is room for everything. For a while, the demons fired more arrows and screamed more vehemently. After a time, they went silent and their spears and arrows turned into flowers, healing ointments and beautiful perfumes. This setback was concerning to Mara, but he had one more trick up his sleeve.

This fragment of the myth teaches us that we need a practice to face difficulties, that our demons are impersonal and we do not have to identify with them. We can cultivate love and compassion toward the parts of ourselves that are most frightening and that we most want to reject.

Duty Calls

Mara then showed Siddhartha visions of the horrible things that were happening because he was not fulfilling his responsibility as the next warrior king. Invaders were killing entire villages on the borders of his father's kingdom. There was mutiny among his father's troops because of lack of leadership. Mara said, *Siddhartha! You are irresponsible. Why are you wasting your time meditating every day? You are so selfish. You should be attending to your responsibilities. You should be taking care of others. You are doing nothing.*

At this point, Siddhartha reached down with his right hand and touched the ground. He said, *I have come to awaken, I take the earth as my witness.*

At that moment, Mara vanished.

Siddhartha did not reach up to the heavens and declare himself enlightened. He reached down to the ground from which we come, to the earth of which we are part. This moment is frequently represented in statues of Buddha. It was the moment of his awakening.

Awakening

Siddhartha, an ordinary person just like you and me, was transformed into an Awakened One. The meaning of *Buddha* is *one who is awake.*

He sat through the night, allowing his realization to unfold.

He sat for a week, enjoying the freedom of being awakened.

The second week, he walked away from the Bodhi tree and looked back upon it to make sense of what had happened.

The third week he spent walking back and forth integrating what had happened. It took him four more weeks to fully understand.

He then contemplated the vast suffering of the world. With his intuitive vision, he saw that people had too much dust in their eyes and would not understand his realizations. He decided not to teach, because it would be pointless. Nobody would understand or care.

Time To Teach

Brahman, the king of the Hindu gods, became concerned that the Buddha did not want to teach, because the gods had long been waiting for the teachings of a Buddha. Brahman took matters into his own hands. He came down from the heavens and bowed to Buddha. He said, *Lord Buddha, we have been waiting for eons and eons. Please look again, and you will see that there are a few with little dust in their eyes.*

Buddha looked again and found this to be true. He also knew intimately the path from suffering to freedom.

There are many beings that stumble into some degree of awakening, but have no idea how they got there, or how to teach others. The mythology says that Buddha had been practicing for countless lifetimes, developing the qualities and the wisdom to become a world teacher.

Buddha thought, *How do I proceed?* He decided to find the five ascetics who had left him at the bank of the river. They were the most likely people to understand his teachings. His intuition revealed to him that they were in the deer park near Banaras, about a ten-day walk away.

He set out and, on the way, met a merchant. This man was startled by the presence of Buddha. Peace emanated from him. He was so at ease. The merchant asked, *What are you? Are you some kind of a god? Are you from heaven?*

Buddha responded, *No, I am no god. I am awake.*

The End of Suffering

After ten days, Buddha arrived at Isipathana, the Deer Park. You can visit there today. It is a few miles north of Varanasi, a green oasis of tranquility in the midst of the cacophony of India.

Buddha approached his five friends, the ascetics. As he approached, they scorned him. They said, *Ha! There is that Gautama guy. He went back to eating. Why would we have anything to do with someone like that?*

But as Buddha approached, they noticed his calmness and peacefulness. He was remarkably present. His eyes had a depth, softness and compassion they had never seen in another person.

They made a seat for him.

Buddha said, *My friends, we have been seeking the end of suffering, and I have found it.*

Suffering

Buddha gave his first sermon, the Dhammacakkappavattana Sutta—which means "Putting in Motion the Wheel of the Dharma"—at the Deer Park to the five ascetics. This teaching was the first time Buddha articulated the Four Noble Truths.

Buddha taught the First Noble Truth, *My friends, there is Dukkha. There is a great deal of suffering, uncertainty and unsettledness in life. This Dukkha is caused by Tanha.*

He taught the Second Noble Truth, *There is Tanha. There is thirst, grasping and craving. There is the tendency in the mind to demand that something be different. There is the grasping after pleasure, security and consistency. There is the pushing away of pain. There is the desperate desire to become something different. There is the drive to accomplish this task and get on with the next one.*

This grasping, my friends, is the cause of suffering.

He taught the Third Noble Truth, *There exists Nirvana, the quenching and extinguishing of suffering.*

At this point, one of the five friends had his first glimpse of awakening. For a moment, the friend's identification with his separate personality ceased. His destiny was sealed. He too would become an awakened one.

The five ascetics were right on the brink. Buddha taught the Fourth Noble Truth, which is the Eightfold Path. Then, he articulated this Noble Truth, the comprehensive teaching that provides a map of how to live one's life to become awakened. This path is explained in Chapter 5.

All it took was Buddha's presence and the teachings of the Four Noble Truths. One by one, his friends became awakened. They became *arhats*, fully awakened beings.

Buddha sent the five arhats in five different directions. Now that they understood the Dharma, the nature of reality, they could teach others.

Buddha had an extraordinary life and effect on the world. He taught for forty-two years, with thousands of followers. The teachings took hold and still exist today, 2,600 years later.

During his long life he experienced great difficulties.

There were two attempts on his life. Both of them came from his jealous cousin, Devadatta. In the first attempt, Devadatta rolled a boulder off a cliff when Buddha was passing below, hoping to kill him. Devadatta tried again in a city with narrow streets. An aggressive male elephant named Nalagiri lived in the city. Devadatta got Nalagiri very drunk and then jabbed him with a spike, which sent the incensed elephant charging down a narrow passage toward Buddha. Buddha's chief attendant, Ananda, was in front of him. With the intention of protecting Buddha with his own life, Ananda commanded, *Move aside, Lord Buddha.* Buddha calmly replied, *I'll take care of this, Ananda.*

As Nalagiri stampeded toward him, Buddha calmly stood and held up his hand. Nalagiri got closer, then skidded to a stop when he encountered *metta*, or love. Nalagiri bowed.

Even though Buddha was fully awakened, there were many challenges.

The Monastic Order and Rules

In fifth-century India it was the custom for men to leave their homes and families and go to the forest to seek liberation—freedom from suffering and enlightenment. It was a time of great social upheaval and questioning. The seekers wandered in the forests and countryside, depending on villagers for food, clothing and medicine. A community gathered rapidly around Buddha. This was the beginning of the Buddhist monastic order.

At first there were few rules. However, because they were dealing with the human mind and behavior, problems soon arose. Over time, as each new problem came up, new rules were created. Ultimately, there were 228 major rules for monks in the Theravada lineage. The Five Precepts, which form the foundation of the Buddhist moral and ethical code, are at the center of these rules. (See Chapter 6.)

Each of the 228 rules for monks has a story about its creation. One of the stories explains the rule that the monks must not travel during the rainy season. This rule arose because of an encounter with the Jains, followers of another great teacher who was alive at the time, named Mahavir.

The Jains were deeply concerned with doing no harm. They wore masks over their mouths and filtered their water, not to protect themselves but to protect the bugs. During the rainy season they did not wander, because bugs and worms crawled onto the paths, and it would become impossible not to kill some when walking.

At that time, Buddha's monks wandered during the rainy season. They couldn't tell where the fields were and sometimes walked across them. The monks were criticized by the Jains for being insensitive to the bugs, and by the villagers for damaging their crops.

Buddha made a rule that each year during the rainy season, the monks would congregate for three months of meditation. This is known as the *vassa*, or the annual rains retreat. This rule provides inspiration for each of us to take some time in retreat.

Other rules were designed to support monks in acting in skillful ways:

- Not to touch money
- To store no food and to live by being dependent daily upon villagers for food and all their requisites
- Not to be alone with a person of the opposite gender.

- No high and lofty beds
- Only eat meat if it was not killed specifically for the monks

Rahula Becomes a Monk

After several years, Buddha went back to Kapilavastu. As he entered the city, his father heard he was coming and he sent a messenger to say, *Do not disgrace me. Don't come into this city dressed in rags and sleeping on the ground. Come to the palace.* Instead, Buddha, went to a forest outside the city boundaries, where he and the monks were welcomed to stay.

Yasodhara, his former wife, sent their thirteen-year old son, Rahula, to him. She said to Rahula, *Go to Buddha and tell him you want your inheritance.* Rahula didn't come back.

Imagine that your thirteen-year-old child goes to visit your former spouse, whom the child has not seen for years, and does not return.

Yasodhara then sent a messenger to ask Buddha to please come to the castle to talk.

No doubt that would have been an interesting conversation!

Out of that meeting came a rule that no son would be allowed to become a monk without the permission of both parents. This was revolutionary at the time, when women were not included in decision making.

Ordaining Women

Soon after that, Queen Prajapati and Yasodhara came to Buddha and asked him to allow women to ordain. They wanted women to have the same opportunity as men to practice deeply and turn toward a monastic life. Yasodhara explained, *We too want to devote ourselves to the practice of Dharma. We'd like to start a monastic order for women.*

Buddha declined.

They came a second time with the same request. He declined again.

Finally, upon the third request, he gave his blessing for the creation of a monastic order for women. The women had not given up. They had persisted in spite of the social constraints that said that women should not even consider becoming part of the monastic life. Buddha was convinced of their sincerity and readiness. Given the status of women in India at the time, this was another revolutionary development.

Queen Prajapati and Yasodhara were the founders of an order of nuns, and both became arhats.

Stepping Out of the Dominant Paradigm

In Buddha's time, the ancient Hindu caste system, which divided people into hierarchical categories based on birth, went unchallenged. In a radical break with this system, Buddha taught that a person's value as a human being did not come from the womb from which he or she was born. He taught that your value as a human has nothing to do with your socioeconomic status, but everything to do with your actions, attitude and intent.

When people became followers of Buddha, they stepped out of the caste system. This was revolutionary at the time, and still is. Even today in India, there is an unofficial caste system in place.

The Wars

It is easy to create a fantasy in which the emergence of Buddha led to a time of unity and peace. It's natural for us to imagine a golden age. It is also natural for us to believe that once people awaken, there will be no more strife in their lives or on the planet. Buddha did not teach this; he knew that he could not cause the cessation of all the conflict around him. Even a person with the stature, compassion and wisdom of Buddha was not able to connect with everyone.

One of Buddha's cousins, a prince, needed a bride. He was promised a princess bride. She was to be sent to him from Kapilavastu. For unknown reasons, the court at Kapilavastu tried to trick him, sending a common girl.

The ruse failed, and the prince became enraged. His pride was wounded. He decided to seek revenge and set out with his army to wage war on Kapilavastu.

When Buddha learned that the prince was on the warpath, he walked to the road that led to Kapilavastu and sat under a scrawny tree in the sun. When the cousin came along, he was startled to see Buddha and exclaimed, *Lord Buddha, what are you doing here? Aren't you hot sitting under that tree that offers so little shade?*

Buddha replied, *No, the proximity of you and my loved ones in Kapilavastu, my family, cools my blood.*

The prince, swayed by Buddha's compassion and love, had a change of heart. He turned his army around and went back.

When he got home, his family and advisors mocked him, *Are you going to let them get away with deceiving and humiliating you?*

We all know the insidious workings of shame. Soon the prince was full of hatred again and his temper got the best of him.

He set off with his army a second time. He encountered Buddha a second time, and once again, Buddha averted the tragedy. The cycle happened a third time, and Buddha realized he couldn't stop it.

Kapilavastu was completely destroyed. There was a vast bloodletting, and everyone in the city was killed.

Human history is littered with cities being destroyed and humans doing terrible things to each other out of hatred, greed and delusion. Why couldn't the Buddha stop this from happening? He understood the depths of ignorance and conditioning that stand between ordinary human beings and waking up. He taught a path for individual awakening, not a social remedy. Many people who met him were unimpressed. They saw him as just another spiritual teacher. Buddha did not take this personally, as he looked upon the world and everyone in it with profound compassion and understanding.

Buddha's Death

Buddha lived eighty-two years, which for that time was remarkable. At the end of his life, he was living in the kingdom of King Bimbisara, who had been a great devotee and benefactor, and had invited Buddha and his monks to live in a forest grove near the city of the king.

When Buddha first arrived at Bimbisara's kingdom, he had many monks in his retinue. Jettavana, a very wealthy person, owned a beautiful grove of trees near Bimbisara's city.

The king approached Jettavana and said, *I would like to buy this grove to provide sanctuary to the Buddha and his followers.*

At first, Jettavana refused. The king countered, *If I bring enough gold coins to cover the entire surface of the ground, would you accept that?* Jettavana accepted.

When Bimbisara's brought the coins, he was one piece short. Jettavana said, *I'll accept that.* In this way, knowingly or unknowingly, Bimbisara gave Jettavana an opening to practice generosity and participate in supporting Buddha.

Buddha and the monks would wander most of the year, but stay in the grove during the rainy seasons. They spent about twenty-five rainy seasons in the grove. King Bimbisara was a great benefactor.

We now come to the end of the story of Buddha's life. Buddha was staying in Jettavana's grove when King Bimbisara's son decided that it was time for the old king to go. As was common in that time, in India and elsewhere, the successor killed his father and ascended to the throne. One of the first actions of the new king was to expel Buddha and his monks from the Jettavana grove.

Buddha left with a small group of monks. The followers dispersed. On foot, walking across the country, Buddha headed for another destination where they might take refuge. He was an old man. He had headaches and his body was wearing out.

At one point in the journey, Buddha fell ill. Ananda pleaded with him, *We need you. Please, use your tremendous energies and make yourself well.* Buddha acceded to this request. He suppressed his sickness and he was well for a little longer. But still, he was very old and very tired.

Along the way, the group stopped in a small village. A man in the village prepared a dinner for Buddha. Unknowingly, the man cooked bad meat, and Buddha got food poisoning. He fell very ill. He was dying.

The monks became angry at the man who had prepared the meal. Buddha told them to calm their anger. He explained that he was grateful to this man, for the man was playing a crucial role in the life of Buddha. Buddha said, *There are two important meals in the life of a Buddha. There is the one just before awakening and the one that allows complete cessation.*

It became clear to the monks that he was dying. Some monks understood the Dharma and were accepting of this natural passing away of Buddha. Others were bereft. In their grief and fear, they urgently asked, *Who will succeed you? Who will guide us?* Buddha's last words were, *Take the Dharma as your refuge. Take no other refuge. Make of yourself a light.*

Then he died.

The Detail That Captures You

Remember that the story of Buddha is partly historical and partly mythological. Mythology is a map of our inner lives.

If you are reading this book, you are already on a spiritual quest and ready to see the story of Buddha as a map of your inner life. Take a moment to pause and reflect. Here are some questions to guide you:

- What detail in this story was particularly alive for you?
- How did that detail resonate with some aspect of your own life?
- Did the story help you make sense of your own longings, hopes or fears?
- What teachers have you encountered and what have you learned from them?
- How has your exploration of self-indulgence, self-mortification and meditation unfolded?
- Does Buddha's story help make sense of some aspect of your spiritual quest?
- How is your quest similar to that of Buddha?

"No One Quite Like Me" Exercise

Make a drawing of a heart on a small piece of paper or find a piece of paper in your favorite color.

On the paper, write those words Siddhartha exclaimed immediately after his own birth: *Heavens above and worlds below, there is no one quite like me.*

If you can, find pictures of yourself as an infant or child and make a collage of them along with the quotation. Put this creation somewhere you will see it each day.

4

The Five Hindrances

MANY PEOPLE, SOMETIMES EVEN long-term meditators, have the misunderstanding that the purpose of meditation is to become a great breath meditator. A great breath meditator, they believe, should be able to control their mind, get rid of all thoughts and emotions, and sit in a blissful empty state focused on the breath. When they can't do that, they become frustrated and often quit meditation.

The disturbances and obstacles that arise in meditation are inevitable. One way to characterize them is as the five hindrances. The path forward is to recognize the hindrances as a normal part of every human mind, learn about them, and use them for your awakening.

The five hindrances are ubiquitous. You can most likely encounter at least one of them right now. You do not need to change anything. Just stay where you are. Set your intention to be aware of what is happening in this moment. Put your timer on for three minutes and keep your mind focused on your breath.

What happened? I bet your mind wandered. Your intention to focus on the breath didn't endure because one or more of the hindrances came into bloom. You may have been carried away in a fantasy of something you would like. Or perhaps some emotionally laden thought about something you don't like overtook you. Maybe your mind started planning or remembering things you need to do. Perhaps you felt sleepy, and even took a little cat nap. Or maybe the entire time you kept thinking you should be doing something useful and productive instead of wasting your time sitting there doing nothing.

All of these thoughts and feelings, and the multitudinous variations of them, are normal in a human consciousness. To be born in a human body with a human mind means you have these experiences. Even Buddha had them after fully awakening. The difference is that when you are awake, you are able to notice the arising of a hindrance and not identify with it, fight against it, chase after it or get carried away by it.

The Five Hindrances

There are lots of helpful lists in Buddhism. They make it easier to categorize, learn and remember on an intellectual level. However, the lists are not the lesson, just as the map is not the territory. The listing of the five hindrances articulates our mental states so we can recognize them.

The Inuit and other cultures that live in the far north have as many as a hundred words for different kinds of snow. Their lives have depended upon being able to perceive and describe this essential element of their environment.

I experienced this when I worked as a ski patrolman in Andermatt, a ski resort at the top of the Swiss Alps where the Gotthard tunnel passes underneath the slopes to cross the border to Italy. Working at high altitude on skis six days a week, in all kinds of weather, through an entire winter on that massive mountain, I encountered many different kinds of snow.

There is the kind of snow that you break through really easily, and there is powdery snow that flows around your body. There is icy snow, which is different from frozen snow. There is slushy snow and cement-like snow. There is sticky snow and snow that looks like a billion little Styrofoam balls, none of them sticking together. As I learned the different kinds of snow, I learned how to ski in different conditions, and how to help others who were lost, stuck or hurt.

When you can name an experience, you can perceive it. Perceiving it, you can observe it carefully. You come to understand it. With understanding, you can learn acceptance. With acceptance, you learn how to live with it, how to make wise decisions about it, and perhaps how to make skillful use of difficult circumstances.

Thus, we start with the five hindrances by naming them. They are:

- Desire—wanting, greed, lust

- Aversion—disliking, anger, hatred

- Restlessness—agitation, worry, remorse, planning
- Sloth and Torpor—sleepiness, dullness, lethargy, being spaced out
- Doubt—suspicion, uncertainty, competing belief systems

The hindrances are of such importance that we need to memorize them so that we have a way of naming our experience when we are confused about what is happening in our meditation. Here is a way to remember them. Imagine the hindrances manifesting as two polarities and a single point. Desire and aversion form one polarity. In desire, we are drawn toward the contents of the mind or some external stimulus. In aversion, the mind dislikes the object and strikes against it. It wants the experience to stop. The second polarity is between sloth and torpor and restlessness. At one end there is too little energy. At the other end there is too much. Standing all by itself is doubt.

An Analogy

Have you been to Crater Lake in Oregon? It is something to behold. A wonder of the world. There is enough water in Crater Lake for every human on the planet to have two thousand six hundred and fifty liters (seven hundred gallons). The explosion that created the crater was a planetary event. The ash from that explosion is two centimeters deep in parts of Saskatchewan, Canada, over a thousand miles away.

You can imagine Crater Lake as a giant teacup filled with rainwater. There are no streams going into it. It is the clearest water in the world. Every day two stewards of the park gather together in a boat on the lake. They lower a little black and white disk into the water. When both of them can no longer see the disk, the water clarity is determined for the day.

Imagine that you are at Crater Lake. Except for the tour boat no boats are allowed on the lake. But you have been given a rare permit to kayak on the lake. You are somehow very special, so you get the permit.

You believe that if you can peer into the depths of Crater Lake when the water is its clearest, you will perceive the ultimate nature of reality and become an awakened being. You are very excited. You spent the night fasting, clarifying your intentions and preparing yourself. Now it is morning and you make your way onto the lake. You are blissed out. *Yes! Today is the day.*

The Hindrance of Desire, Wanting, Greed, Lust

Gingerly, and with great reverence, you climb into your kayak. You are mindful about every movement. You paddle out to the middle of the lake where it is deepest. You lean over the side of the boat.

The entire lake is suddenly filled with exquisite psychedelic colors. You look a bit longer and see a beautiful white sand beach with gentle waves and a hammock in the shade just for you. After a while you see the perfect job and a loving and devoted partner. Then comes a fantastic meal, an exquisite vintage of wine and a beautiful and delicious pastry. The latest mobile device is delivered to your door, and it's amazing. You are presented with an award for being the best in the world and everyone is applauding you. You are rich, famous, beautiful, incredibly successful and loved by everybody.

You are having a direct encounter with desire, lust and craving.

All the things you could possibly want are in the lake. It is beautiful. You hang around a bit, but ultimately you are disappointed. It was supposed to be your day for awakening, not for hedonism. You have been taught to recognize the hindrance of desire, lust and craving, and can see that today they are present and will not disband. You turn around and paddle back. You know you have four more days left on your permit.

The Hindrance of Aversion, Hatred, Anger

The next morning you wake up early. You go out on the lake at dawn. You have dealt with yesterday's disappointment. You are calm and hopeful. With great care you climb into the kayak. Again, you think, *today is the day.*

You paddle out to the middle of the lake. This time, just as you are about to lean over the side of the boat, the entire lake starts to boil. Yellow sulfur gas bubbles up everywhere, clouding the water. It is terribly uncomfortable. It stings your eyes and stinks.

You paddle a little to the south to see if the water is clearer there. When you look in, you see a replay of all your past traumas and hurts. It is excruciating. You paddle to the west, hoping the water is clear there. Instead, when you look in you see all the things in your life you wish were different. The sight leaves you feeling polluted. Losing heart, you decide to try the north. When you look into the water there, all your worries about the future flood into your vision, one after the other, on a continual spiral. You take a deep breath to re-center yourself and decide to give it one more go. On the east side, instead of clarity you see visions of the people, situations and circumstances that bring on annoyance, anger and fury.

This is aversion, disliking and hatred. You looked over the side of the boat and there was no awakening. You recognize what you are seeing.

You sigh deeply, and paddle to the shore of Crater Lake. There are three more days left on your permit. Three more chances.

The Hindrance of Restlessness, Agitation, Worry

The third day dawns. You get up early again and are climbing into the kayak as the sun blazes over the rim of the lake. You notice each movement of your body as it gets into the boat. You paddle slowly to the middle, not in any rush. As you paddle, your excitement mounts. You are pretty sure today is the day.

Slowly, you put the paddle into the boat. Slowly, you look over the side. Just as you are looking over, a gust of wind blows across the water. You quickly pull the paddle out to steady the boat. As you do, the gust turns into a steady powerful wind. Your excitement is collapsing. You look into the water. There are great whitecaps everywhere. There is no way to see in.

No sooner have your eyes settled on one whitecap then another takes its place. In a series of whitecaps, bobbing up and down, you see all your worries about your job, financial future, and paying the rent. In another series, you see your concerns about your health, your body shape, your diet and getting old. More whitecaps arise full of worries about your partner, children, pets and parents. It's a never-ending show of all the things that stress you out.

You know that that this is restlessness, agitation and worry. It is the mind that cannot settle down. The mind that jumps around.

You didn't become enlightened today. You did not even get a moment of peace. Instead, all you got was whitecaps. You paddle back to shore. Your permit is good for two more days, and you feel fairly confident you will see the great hidden truth tomorrow. After all, pretty much everything that could cloud the water already has, hasn't it?

The Hindrance of Sloth and Torpor

It's early the next morning. You find yourself out on the lake again. Maybe you are not as mindful as you were the last three days because you can't quite remember how you got there, but you are mindful in the moment. Maybe you are a little less excited because there have been some disappointments, but you still believe that today is the day.

You arrive at the middle of the lake where it is deepest and look over the side. Somehow Crater Lake is suddenly like the Colorado River in full flood. You can't see even a millimeter down. It is the color of mud.

Your mind goes numb and you space out. It's like a great fogginess has overtaken you. A feeling of laziness and dullness overcomes you. You are awake but there is no presence. It's like someone is home but the lights are not on. You feel like you are the mud.

This is sloth and torpor. Over the course of your training, you have become very familiar with it, and learned to recognize it.

You turn the boat around to see if a new perspective will make a difference. Looking over the side, you notice that the mud color changes from brown to grey. As you are looking, you notice your head bobbing into sleep and your mouth gape open. Embarrassed, you pull yourself awake again. As soon as you do, your eyes start to droop and, like a curtain going down in your head, you feel pulled into sleepiness.

Sighing, you pull yourself together and paddle back to shore. Your permit is still good for one more day. You make your way back to camp, eat and settle down for the night.

The Hindrance of Doubt

It is dawn and you are well rested. Today is the last day of your permit. You resolve to do everything in your power to become enlightened today. You have practiced for years. You have this special permit. Today must be the day.

Renewing your sense of awe and feeling of solemnity, you mindfully climb into the boat, and mindfully paddle out, taking note of each time the paddle arches into the water, then out of the water. You arrive at the middle. You take three deep slow breaths.

You look over the side.

There are pond weeds everywhere. The whole lake is thick with milfoil. Tears come to your eyes, clouding your vision. You wipe them away and look again. In the milfoil you see visions of disbelief. The truth is being revealed by people with clear minds and credentials. You look a little further out, and it becomes clear in your mind that the whole thing is chicanery. It was all tricks and manipulation. You cast your eyes to the left, and it becomes clear that everyone who believes that enlightenment is possible is delusional. They have lost touch with reality, and so have you with this stupid trip. To the right, when you look into the weeds, you decide that it's utterly useless and definitely time to go home.

This is doubt. You have been trained and are able to recognize it. You paddle back, noticing the thoughts of doubt that arise. On the shore, you join the others who came with you on this journey and share your experience.

Make No War

It is very easy to make the hindrances into enemies and battle against them. It is common to think that you can get rid of them. The hindrances are not enemies. Anger, hatred, desire, worry, restlessness, sloth, torpor and doubt are the experiences of every human mind. Making enemies of them is akin to thinking of your hand as the enemy because it opened that box of chocolates and put them in your mouth.

The first time I did a two-month retreat, I remember sitting at a desk and being aware that the mind was restless. I thought I would get rid of restlessness on that retreat, forever. I never succeeded. It is still here. It's the same with the other hindrances. However, they have changed in intensity and duration. More importantly, my relationship to them is different now. I am less identified with them. I am confident they will pass.

I experience the hindrances as impersonal and do not have to react to them. Just as I do not try to change the outer weather, I can accept the inner weather.

Here is a story to illustrate a healthy attitude towards the five hindrances. A large family is having its annual family reunion. Every year they rent a beautiful large beach house on the Oregon coast. This year they gather in the winter because of some family circumstances. It rains every day. The wind blows and it is cold. The children are complaining, but the grandmother is happy and smiling. Every morning and afternoon she goes for a walk on the beach. They ask her how she can be so happy. She replies, *If it's going to rain, I may as well accept it and have a good time.* The story is a metaphor for the Noble Truths and the end of suffering.

The Core Strategy

The core strategy for working with the hindrances is to observe them. When you do, you recognize they are impermanent and not personal. A hindrance arises and then disappears. Feelings arise, stay around for a while, then disappear. Thoughts come and go. This is the human mind in action.

Now that you have an idea of how to identify and name the five hindrances, you will find that one or more of them arises with regularity. Sylvia Boorstein, one of the elder teachers at Spirit Rock Meditation Center in California, coined a colorful phrase: *multiple hindrance attacks*. Sometimes three or four hindrances at a time will assail you. Over time, and with practice, you will identity patterns or themes. Some of the patterns will dissolve with noticing them. Others will take a long time to dissolve.

Mindfulness of Desire

Desire is a necessary and integral part of us as human beings. Without desire, we would not seek to fulfill many of our needs. We would not be drawn to eat, seek shelter or create life or art. Our species would not exist without desire. You would die within a few days without the desire to drink water or sleep and a few weeks without the desire to eat. Our intention is not to get rid of desire, but to become conscious of it and not be a slave to it.

When desire arises in the mind, there is attraction to the objects that arise at the sense doors. These can be in the form of pleasant thoughts, sounds, smells or visual objects. One wants more of them, and the mind can become obsessed with strategies for grasping and owning the object of desire.

Today's culture of consumerism is based on the belief that happiness comes from the satisfaction of desire. There is little or no honoring of conscious restraint or renunciation as important factors in the pursuit of happiness. Despite countless experiences of increased consumption failing to satisfy us, we continue to pursue that dead end. To free ourselves from being slaves to consumerism and desire, we bring mindfulness to the experience of desire itself. Imagine you are sitting in meditation and the desire arises to get up and have a cup of tea and a cookie, read the text message you just got or check your email. Without mindfulness, it is likely that you will do these things without thinking about it. Practicing mindfulness allows you to observe the process of the arising of desire and its eventual passing away.

This exercise allows you to see the arising of desire. With mindfulness, you notice when there is that tension in the body that comes from desire. You develop your capacity to be aware of it and to decide if acting on the desire would be wise or harmful. You realize that desires have a natural life cycle and that they arise and can pass away if not acted upon. As you develop this capacity to exercise restraint with less significant desires, you learn skillfulness with more difficult ones.

Ultimately, you will come to the freedom of recognizing the impersonal and impermanent nature of desire.

Aversion Exercise

As with desire, aversion is part of who we are as mammals. It is essential. Without aversion, we would not pull our hand back from a flame or run from the charging bear. When aversion develops into anger, it mobilizes our energy to defend ourselves and our loved ones.

The mind in aversion strikes against the objects that arise at the sense doors. It wants less of them or wants them to cease completely.

While aversion plays an important role in our survival, if we cannot work with it skillfully it can lead us to lives that are filled with dissatisfaction and conflict. If we cannot mindfully identify and moderate aversion and disliking in our minds, we cannot cultivate the essential capacities of love, empathy and compassion that are also basic parts of our nature.

As with desire and the other hindrances, you cannot stop the aversion from arising, but you can free yourself from having to struggle with it or act it out.

Aversion arises as disliking, negative judgment or hatred. When this happens, pause and turn directly toward the experience. You will likely notice tension in the body and a flood of aversive thoughts. Aversion can be a hot fire. Notice how convincing it is, how the mind justifies the fact of disliking. Notice any "enemy" images that arise in the mind. Feel carefully where in your body the sensations of aversion occur. This can take place on your meditation cushion or anywhere in your life. Take the time to connect very intimately with the aversive images. Every time awareness of aversion arises, and you note the experience in your body or the thoughts and feelings in your mind, you take one more step away from being a slave to aversion. Congratulate yourself each time you become aware of aversion in your mind and body. In this way, you strengthen your capacity for mindfulness, wisdom and compassion.

Restlessness and Agitation Manifesting as Impatience Exercise

Restlessness, agitation and worry are states that share in common the trait of the mind jumping around from one object to another. There are many manifestations of this hindrance. Impatience is a kind of restlessness mixed with aversion. When you are meditating, impatience may arise with thoughts like, *I want this to be over. I want to get back to work. There is so much to do and I will feel better if I get it done.* In daily life, impatience may arise when you are stuck in traffic, in line at a grocery checkout, or your browser is taking a long time to load.

Patience is born only through consciously suffering impatience. If you want to be more patient, when impatience arises observe the mind wanting things to be different. Note that this is restlessness. Notice the physical experience of restlessness. Notice how the restlessness is different or weakens when there is awareness of it, even if the awareness lasts for just a moment. You can use circumstances that would normally give rise to restlessness, like traffic or any long wait, to practice working with this hindrance mindfully, and experience liberation in any moment. Over time, you will discover yourself spontaneously resting easily in the present moment as it is, including the experience of restlessness and agitation.

Concentration is an antidote to restlessness. In your meditation you might try gently focusing more precisely on the beginning and ending of each breath to clarify your focus.

Sloth and Torpor Exercise

Sloth and torpor manifest as sleepy dullness and a tendency to go unconscious. They will sometimes arise even when you are well rested. Sometimes the mind falls into sloth and torpor when something is emerging in it that is unacceptable or unbearable.

When sloth and torpor arise, you have a tremendous opportunity to clearly observe the truth of non-self (*anatta*). You may be sitting in meditation and discover your head falling forward. Despite your best efforts, you may discover that you can't stay awake, and that you keep dropping into something like sleep.

When you discover that sloth and torpor are arising in your meditation, set your intention to stay wide awake for the next two minutes. In all likelihood, you will fall into sloth and torpor within seconds. Notice that each time the head falls forward, or the jaw drops open, the sense of self, ego, or *I* disappears. In other words, the *I* is gone. Then, in the middle of being deeply unconscious, the mystery of mindfulness happens. Suddenly, awareness arises again. With being awake, the *I* reappears. Where did the *I* go? Why can't you control the mind and stay awake?

The *I* that made the decision to stay conscious lasted briefly then disappeared. Then it reappeared. The *I* was not around to wake itself up. That happened all by itself. This can happen multiple times in a few minutes. The *I* vanishes twenty times. The *I* reappears. Gone. Back. Gone. Back. The *I* is not in charge. It wants to be, but it is not.

This is not a failure in meditation. It is an opportunity for insight. It is possible to have profound insight into the nature of self and reality through mindfulness of sloth and torpor.

Strategies to try when enveloped by sloth and torpor include sitting in bright light with your eyes open, standing to practice or doing walking meditation.

Doubt Exercise

Throughout your meditation practice, you may be visited periodically by doubt. Other descriptors of this state are despair, dispiritedness and depression. You may doubt the practice, yourself, your teacher, others who meditate and the teachings. Sometimes this doubt can become extreme. In some mystical traditions, severe doubt attacks have been called the dark night of the soul. I call doubt *the practice killer*. When doubt hits, it can really hit hard. Strong doubt can deflect you from your spiritual path.

When doubt arises, the first way to work with it is to recognize it for what it is. It is hard to do this because doubt is very convincing. Doubt says, *This is the truth*. Ask yourself which of the hindrances is present. Often there will be two or more hindrances acting together. The Buddha taught that the company of good friends is a strong antidote for doubt. When you can, speak with your teacher, meditation buddies or other people who meditate. They can help you recognize doubt for what it is. The act of recognizing doubt as a hindrance and talking about it will often result in deepening your confidence in the Dharma.

Many years ago, when I was on retreat with my teacher, Ruth Denison, doubt hit me hard. Suddenly, I knew with certainty that Ruth was a fraud, meditation was a delusion and Buddhism was a cult. My entire psychotherapy practice was based on Buddhist psychology. This meant that my professional life was based on a delusion and my livelihood was at stake. I would have to go home and start everything over again.

This doubt manifested as existential anguish. There was terrible confusion and utter uncertainty about how to proceed. I wanted to leave the retreat right then, but I had been practicing with Ruth for a long time, and had been teaching for a number of years and I felt I had to say goodbye to her before leaving.

This experience was even more painful because early in my Buddhist training I had fallen into a Buddhist cult where I spent five years under the influence of a teacher who was charismatic, narcissistic, manipulative and dangerous. I feared that I had once again fallen into a mind control group.

I crept out of the meditation hall and went for a walk in the woods. After a while, it occurred to me to ask myself the questions that I usually asked meditation students when they came to me in crisis. The first question was, *What is happening right now? What hindrances are present?* I contemplated desire. Yes, there was a desire to get out of there. *Was there aversion?* Yes, there was great aversion to Ruth, to the retreat and to the teachings. *What about agitation?* Yes, there was agitation. *How about sloth and torpor?* No. None of that was present. Then I considered doubt. Ah ha! I became aware that doubt was present and predominant in my mind. This realization was like a tiny seed of transformation. The recognition of the state of doubt opened the door to a different way of being with the feelings and thoughts of doubt. As I continued walking, the doubt melted away and opened into ease and a new level of faith and confidence in Ruth as my teacher and in the Dharma as a vehicle for my awakening.

The Manure of Awakening

One of the first Tibetan teachers to bring Buddhism to the West, Chogyam Trungpa, said, *The hindrances are the manure out of which you create your awakening.* Once you know how to be curious, and pay mindful attention to the five hindrances, you will discover how ubiquitous they are. Most of the time when you sit down to meditate, or when you practice mindfulness in your daily life, they will appear in some form or another. By compassionately and patiently attending to them you will transform them into your awakening.

5

The Eightfold Path,
or the Path to Happiness

My friends, let's grow up.
Let's stop pretending we don't know the deal here.
Or if we truly haven't noticed, let's wake up and notice.
Look: Everything that can be lost, will be lost.
It's simple—how could we have missed it for so long?
Let's grieve our losses fully, like ripe human beings,
But please, let's not be so shocked by them.
Let's not act so betrayed,
As though life had broken her secret promise to us.
Impermanence is life's only promise to us,
And she keeps it with ruthless impeccability.
To a child she seems cruel, but she is only wild,
And her compassion exquisitely precise:
Brilliantly penetrating, luminous with truth,
She strips away the unreal to show us the real.
This is the true ride—let's give ourselves to it!
Let's stop making deals for a safe passage:
There isn't one anyway, and the cost is too high.
We are not children anymore.
The true human adult gives everything for what cannot be lost.
Let's dance the wild dance of no hope!

—JENNIFER WELWOOD, *POEMS FOR THE PATH*

MOST OF US DO not set out on the journey of the Eightfold Path until we become aware that our usual strategies for happiness are failing. We spend much of our lives attempting to achieve happiness and security and they prove remarkably elusive. At some point, for some of us, it becomes apparent that pursuing the conventional experiences and symbols of success leaves us feeling empty or unsatisfied. The truth of impermanence begins to dawn within us. Jennifer Welwood's poem quoted here is like a splash of cold water waking us up. It invites us to turn our dissatisfaction into a quest: to set off on the Eightfold Path.

A Cut Gemstone

Imagine the Eightfold Path as an exquisite gem that is polished with eight facets. If you shine a light into one facet, it illuminates all the others. Practicing one dimension of the path will strengthen the others. In this way the path is not linear. It is instead circular, with each step on the way leading further inward toward wisdom, compassion and love.

The eight facets are:

- Wise view (or wise understanding)
- Wise intention
- Wise action
- Wise speech
- Wise livelihood
- Wise effort
- Wise mindfulness
- Wise concentration

We use the word "wise" because living our lives aligned with this model leads to happiness. We can also use the word "skillful" in this context.

The Eightfold Path, as with all Buddha's teachings, is not to be taken as dogma or something one must believe. Instead, it can be used as an hypothesis to test. Is it true? Does it work? It is an experiment to try out. If it brings you freedom and happiness, you will know that it works. What begins as a collection of interesting ideas ultimately becomes a known truth upon which you can rely.

This chapter is illustrated with stories that show how following the Eightfold Path can lead to happiness and tranquility.

If you decide to follow the Eightfold Path, you will find that the more deeply you practice and learn about mindfulness, the more it will integrate into all aspects of your life. You will also discover that when you fall away from it, you can easily come back to it. It will become a refuge from suffering.

Buddha's Metaphor

After Buddha's awakening, his first teaching, as mentioned in Chapter 3, was given to five friends who became fully awakened themselves. He taught them the Four Noble Truths, the fourth of which is the Eightfold Path. He began with a metaphor.

Imagine if someone fired an arrow into your left side, and the arrow was sticking in you. Would you be in pain? This is not a trick question. Yes. You would.

If someone then fired a second arrow into your right side, would there be more suffering?

The Buddha taught that the first arrow is the inevitable pain and discomfort of life. Pain is inherent to human life and cannot be avoided. The second arrow represents the suffering that arises because of our non-acceptance of life as it is. Buddha taught that the second arrow is our resistance and reactivity to the first arrow. Our task is to awaken to the second arrow, to remove it, and to live life on its own terms rather than as a constant struggle.

Three Steps to Knowledge

Each of the Four Noble Truths can be understood in three steps. These three steps are also called insights. The three insights come through three levels of understanding.

The first step is to understand intellectually. The second step entails the direct experience of the truth as it manifests in your life. The third step arises as you gain mastery and integrate intellectual and experiential understanding. You begin to embody and know the truth.

The First Noble Truth: Pain and Suffering

Our lives inevitably contain pain that arises from birth, sickness, old age, decay and death. Life also includes four categories of disappointing experiences that happen to all of us:

- Being with people we do not want to be with
- Not being with the people we want to be with
- Having experiences we do not want to have
- Not having experiences we want to have

These disappointing experiences are inevitable and ubiquitous. They happen every day.

By reading this chapter, you have come to intellectually understand the First Noble Truth. This understanding is step one in knowing the First Noble Truth. The second step can be taken when you experience the next painful event in your life. Something disappointing or painful will happen. You will learn to turn toward this suffering or dukkha without flinching. You will turn toward it and bear it as a wagon bears a load. This bearing with dukkha is an experiential learning. It will change you. You will grow in your capacity to bear with, rather than flee into distraction.

As I write these words, it has been about a month since I had the first symptoms of a cold and the sickness lingers. In the afternoon my throat still closes, and in the evening it is difficult to breathe. The reason I got sick is not because I did something wrong or there was something wrong with me. The reason I got sick is not because I had bad or wrong thoughts. Human beings get sick. Ultimately, we get sick, and then we die, unless we die some other way. One hundred and thirty thousand people will die today on our planet. Birth, sickness, old age, decay and death are unavoidable. The four categories of disappointing experiences listed above are unavoidable.

This is the first arrow. This is the First Noble Truth. There really is pain in life, no matter what we believe or do.

We use the term *Noble* because when we come to deeply know the Four Noble Truths, we become compassionate, loving and wise.

The Second Noble Truth: The Cause of Suffering

The human mind often does not accept things as they are. It says, *I want more pleasure, success and happiness. I will not accept the reality of this moment. I don't want this pain, discomfort and disappointment. I want it my way. I want to become something different.* Whenever there is resistance to the way things are, there is suffering. Resistance to reality is the second arrow. Our non-acceptance of the way things are causes our suffering.

As with the First Noble Truth, the Second Noble Truth is understood in three steps.

The first step is to understand it intellectually. You learn the concept that resisting the inevitable pain of life is the cause of suffering.

The second step of insight comes with direct experience. Something disappointing or painful happens, and you observe the mind wanting things to be different. Suffering exists, and it is real. In that instant, you consciously experience suffering coming from your not accepting the way things are. You then develop your ability to be conscious of the connection between suffering and non-acceptance. You also recognize that the suffering is separate from pain or disappointing experiences. You train yourself to bear the pain or disappointment and develop your capacity to know how dukkha, or suffering, is created. In this way, over time you become capable of bearing experiences that previously would have been unbearable.

The third step in understanding the Second Noble Truth comes when the realization that suffering arises from non-acceptance of the way things are becomes part of your worldview and psychology. Then you have fully understood the Second Noble Truth. This understanding becomes your automatic thought response when painful experiences arise. Something painful will inevitably happen, causing you to feel sad, angry or upset. But at the same time, an important thought co-arises in the mind. It says something like, *Oh, this mind is wishing for things to be different from what they are.* This is when the Second Noble Truth has become part of you and begins to affect your every experience.

You can test the functional usefulness of this Noble Truth with a theory: to the degree you resist the way things are, suffering arises. The next time you are suffering, ask yourself, *Am I demanding something to be different?* Does this help to illuminate the difference between suffering and its cause? Is this theory accurate and true to your experience?

The Third Noble Truth: The Cessation of Suffering

The Third Noble Truth is that there is relief from suffering. Buddha called this relief *nirvana*. There is great misunderstanding of this word. Often it is thought to mean something like heaven, or an altered state that is somehow otherworldly. Actually, it is a state very natural to us as humans that we can actively cultivate.

The Third Noble Truth is the cessation and quenching of suffering. You pull out the second arrow. You cease demanding that things be different than they are. This does not mean the first arrow disappears—pain may persist. But suffering diminishes and eventually can be totally extinguished.

Buddha had headaches. He experienced the pains of birth, sickness, old age, decay and death just like everyone else. He probably had countless experiences that most anyone would rather not have and was around people most of us would rather not be around. Such pains and disappointments are the conditions of existence, and, in fact, Buddha's life ended painfully by food poisoning. But did he suffer? That is a different question.

Like the other Noble Truths, the Third Noble Truth is first understood intellectually. You first learn the theory and come to an understanding that it is possible to reduce and eventually end suffering.

Then comes the direct experience of the truth of nirvana. Many meditators first experience the truth of nirvana while sitting in meditation. My first glimpse occurred on a retreat in India. For the first time, I committed myself to sitting very still for long periods of time. The teacher sat in front of the group and we would sit for an hour. As the days passed and we repeatedly sat in this way, my right knee began to really bother me. It hurt more and more. I struggled with it. Sometimes my mind would get very freaked out and I was on the verge of panic. *Why am I doing this? This is stupid. When is he going ring the bell? Oh no, my knee is being injured. Oh no, I will have a limp for the rest of my life.* As soon as the sitting was over, and I stood up, the pain was gone. There was no injury to my knee. The pain itself got all mixed up with my psychological reactions to it. I was in pain *and* suffering. I was instructed to turn awareness to the upsetness in the mind, to notice how the fear, anger and disliking were different from the actual sensations. In the middle of one particularly difficult bout with this suffering, suddenly something changed. The suffering was gone. I was no longer panicking, resisting or dreading anything. This was a huge relief. I had been paying very close attention to the suffering and the pain at the moment the suffering vanished. Much to my dismay it came back in force just a few moments later. This really got my attention. I knew that something of importance had just happened. As the days of the retreat passed, it became clear to me that the suffering was different from the sensations of pain. This was a revolutionary discovery. This was the beginning of my understanding of nirvana or the quenching of suffering.

This realization of the causality and extinguishing of suffering is counterintuitive and goes against basic mammalian nature. When we have done all that we can to eliminate pain by all the usual means and it remains, then we turn awareness intentionally right into the pain. We stop trying to change or to get away from the pain. We feel our way to the heart of the painful emotions or pain in the body. We observe the actual direct experience of the suffering and pain. We learn not to flinch or to turn away. We observe all the mental gyrations and thoughts.

Doing this somehow mysteriously allows the discovery that suffering is extra. You learn to relax into the painful sensations and find a remarkable peace. At first this is very difficult, then over time you will learn to use this strategy to suffer less and less and to deal with whatever suffering comes your way.

The Bank Story

It was Tuesday morning. I was tired. I checked my email and saw a flood of alert messages from service providers. One came from an event management company that I use for my classes and which I pay automatically using a credit card. I had been away, teaching a week-long workshop at Breitenbush Hot Springs, an off-the-grid retreat center in the mountains, and had missed the urgent emails. The event management company had cancelled my events, including a class I had scheduled for that night.

I called the bank and the first service representative was not very helpful. I was patient. I was confident that the problem would be easily solved. After a while, the representative let me know the credit card had been shut down. That seemed odd because there was a $9,000 credit limit on it. He would not tell me any more information. I waited a bit, and then called back. The woman who answered put me on hold. I was on hold for thirty minutes. Normally I would be fine with that. There is always stuff to do. As my teacher, Ruth Denison, put it, *Dahlink, once you have the Dharma you never have to wait again, there is always something to attend to.*

But it started to bug me. A very familiar and uncomfortable feeling of irritation began to emerge. Anger started to rear its ugly head. I was tired and short on time to prepare for my class that night.

I have a history of negative experiences with banks, which contributed to my upset. During the economic crash of 2008, my partner and I lost a house and half of our life savings due to the unethical and slimy actions of a bank.

It was quite a painful experience at the time. Now, when the memory of the loss comes up, if the circumstances are right, this story from my personal history can feed the emergence of anger and fear.

Eventually, the woman came back on the line and told me that the bank had been using another company to process the credit cards, but that they had recently started processing credit cards in-house. My payment had been on time, but it had gone to the wrong address and was not credited to my account. The bank had further mistakenly recorded the card as cancelled. It was a bank error.

I watched a whirlwind of negative thoughts and feelings spiraling around inside me. The Buddhist term for this is *papañca,* or mental proliferation. The negative thoughts and feelings whirl about, growing bigger and bigger, consuming you. I was more and more irritated. It was very unpleasant. While this was going on, I remembered living with those kinds of thoughts and feelings a lot in the past.

At this point, I was conscious that the thoughts and feelings were emerging because the circumstances had piled up just so. My consciousness of the suffering did not alleviate the feelings of suffering—I was really irritated—but my perspective helped keep me from acting out my anger on the woman. I told her, *I know that this is not your doing, but I am feeling angry and frustrated. I want you to know that this anger has nothing to do with you, but I really need you to fix this problem because it has bearing on a class I am teaching tonight.* However, she could not fix the bank error.

In the middle of it all, I went to my meditation spot and sat for a while. It was a relief to assume my familiar meditation posture and an internal position of observing rather than being so involved in all the mental activity.

A colleague of mine works at the same bank. I called her and explained the problem. Two hours later, she called back. She had reactivated the card, but it would take two days for it to function again.

My head spun.

I lost it. I ranted, *How come? Do I charge the bank for problems? What about the cost of my time?*

She was great. She said, *Between you and me, this problem you are having with the bank, I have every day, all day, with this bank.*

I apologized for my outburst, and we both had a good laugh. Nevertheless, as soon as I hung up, a whirlwind of negative feelings—more papañca—came up. My gut was tight.

Over and over, the whirlwind of anger, irritation, frustration and confusion stormed up, then subsided. I watched the storms rise and part throughout the day. That evening, on my way to work, I passed the bank. I could feel a growl come up in me. The story the mind was telling started again, *This is the bank that charges me $35 every time I make a late payment or have any problem. How come I can't charge them $35? It's not fair!*

At the same time, there was awareness. *Wow, this is happening again.* A trivial event had turned into an inner anger storm. A couple of times during that day, the thought arose, *Wait a minute—you could be homeless, hungry and sick with no access to medical care. This is not a big deal.* But these are cognitive thoughts. They are separate from the emotional storm. The storm was happening right then, in the heart and in the gut, and it was not listening to reason.

The story ends with a friend saving the day by using one of her credit cards.

This anecdote from everyday life shows how something relatively trivial can cause great suffering. The credit card failure caused by the bank's error was the first arrow, a demonstration of the First Noble Truth in everyday life. Little things can happen that our mind will use to bring us to a place where we feel self-righteous about our anger, hatred or aversion. Then we can act out in ways that we later feel horrible about.

Without awareness, the credit card story could have unfolded into ugly action and an unwholesome experience. I could have verbally abused the people on the other end of the phone. Then, later, I would have felt shame. I would have had remorse, *Oh, I wish I had not done that.*

It is out of this kind of craziness that we often commit harmful actions. Little things trigger us. We emotionally attack people. Then they attack back. Great harm is done to a relationship. Wars emerge.

However, when we understand the Four Noble Truths, an awareness arises about these feelings and thoughts, and we learn how to not cause suffering.

Let's come back to the Eightfold Path, the last of the Four Noble Truths.

Without freedom from suffering, we get caught in the vicious cycle of causing more and more pain to ourselves and others. Through non-acceptance and rejection of how things are, the second arrow cuts deeper and deeper wounds. We suffer greatly.

But the second arrow, the desire for things to be different from the way they are, is not necessary. It is learned and habitual, but it is not required. We can pull out the second arrow and realize the Third Noble Truth, the end of suffering.

The Fourth Noble Truth: The Eightfold Path

The Fourth Noble Truth is the Eightfold Path. It is an exquisite model of how to live our lives in a way that we suffer less and become more loving and compassionate. The Eightfold Path leads to true happiness.

You could to look upon the Four Noble Truths and Eightfold Path as a diagnosis and treatment plan. The first truth points out that there is a disease: suffering. The cause of this disease is the second truth: craving, the mind's demand for reality to be different. The third truth about the ending of suffering is the cure: nirvana, the quenching of the craving for things to be different. Finally, the Eightfold Path is the treatment plan that can result in the ultimate cure.

The rest of this chapter gives you a broad overview of the Eightfold Path. It is a map, and not the territory itself. To explore the territory, experiment with the teachings of the Eightfold Path, applying them to everyday life.

The Eightfold Path's Three Sections

The Eightfold Path is divided into three sections.

- Wisdom: wise view and wise intention; concerned with worldview, understanding, values and intentions.
- Behavior: wise speech, wise action and wise livelihood; concerned with our behavior in everyday life.
- Mental development and wisdom: wise effort, wise concentration and wise mindfulness; concerned with training the mind to become mindful and present in every moment of our lives.

Wise View on the Eightfold Path

The first facet of the Eightfold Path is wise view. It is also called wise understanding, and sometimes right view or right understanding. Wise view means our perception of the world is in keeping with the world as it is, and we do not create suffering. With wise view, we come to see all things as they really are, and to act with such wisdom that we do not cause suffering.

It is extremely difficult to perceive the world as it actually is. Rather than seeing it accurately our perceptions are colored by our hopes and fears, family conditioning, experiences of safety and trauma during our lifetimes, our education and cultural conditioning. These all contribute to a worldview, or perceptual bias, that warps our view of the world. Wise view, when developed, allows us to see things as they really are, independent of our conditioning.

Major elements of wise view are:

- the Four Noble Truths

- the three characteristics of existence

- the law of karma

The Three Characteristics of Existence

The Buddha observed that every phenomenon in the universe has three central characteristics. They are:

- *Anicca* (impermanence): Nothing lasts. Everything with a beginning has an ending. Everything is impermanent, unstable and unpredictable.

- *Dukkha* (suffering or unsatisfactoriness): Being a human is difficult. We can never get enough of what we want, or it never lasts long enough. We get sick and old. There is stress, anxiety and depression. We lose people, pets and things we love. Our dreams and hopes get shattered.

- *Anatta* (non-self, non-soul): Our experience of an enduring self is inaccurate. The self is a subjective experience created in the mind. The truth of anatta is the realization that we are not what we think we are. Awakening to this is liberation.

The concept of anatta is the crown jewel of Buddha's teachings. This does not mean you do not have an ego, body or mind that is different from everyone else, but that these structures are temporary and ultimately do not define who you are. The idea of a drop of water falling into a great ocean is the perfect analogy. The individual separate drop upon falling into the ocean and returning to the whole may realize, *Oh my goodness, I am everything—what a relief.* Across traditions there are different vocabularies, but mystics in all traditions have had the same experience. It is indescribable but understood with experience. Anicca, dukkha and anatta are the three primary characteristics of the universe.

To cultivate wise view, ask yourself the following: Are these three characteristics of existence true? Is there anything permanent, or is everything impermanent? Can permenant satisfaction be found in pleasurable experiences? Can you find an enduring self, or is the self a process, a part of nature and the unfolding universe? Mindfulness practice is a journey in which you look ever more closely at reality. With mindfulness you take your exploration into direct experience and go beneath theories and ideas. As you do so the three characteristics of reality reveal themselves as true beyond all doubt.

Karma

Another dimension of wise view is the law of karma.

This ancient teaching is deeply misunderstood and misused in the West. It is confused with sin, punishment and divine retribution. In its most egregious form, people are asked what they have done to bring some form of illness or tragedy on themselves. This is not what the Buddha taught.

The Buddha spoke of karma as *the light of the world* because it is through understanding this reality of cause and effect that we can shape a destiny rather than live out a fate. Traditional Buddhism has a worldview complete with past and future lives, heavens and hells. There are beliefs about acting in good ways to be sure one is born in a good life next time. I don't know about past and future lives. However, I am convinced that how I respond to the circumstances I find myself in moment by moment has an influence upon what happens in the next moment. My actions have impacts or results.

Here is a way of understanding the law of karma that may be useful to you. In this and every moment you are experiencing the ripening of the fruit of an infinite number of prior conditions. Some of them are personal, some are geologic, some are political and some are genetic. However this moment has come to be, it is what exists right now. It is the reality of this moment. There is no way to really understand how it came to be like this. It is infinitely complex. However, with mindfulness it is possible to be radically awake to the realities of the present moment and the range of possible choices and actions that present themselves. Without this awareness one is doomed to react to present circumstances in instinctive or habitual ways repeating past patterns. With mindfulness you cultivate a space between the impulse to act and the action. You develop a response rather than a reaction. This space allows you to contemplate the likely fruits of your actions and to modulate and shape the intentions that guide the action. Each action conditions the next result.

With this understanding, it becomes clear that moment by moment we choose the course of our lives. This is the law of karma in action.

Wise Intention on the Eightfold Path

The second facet of the Eightfold Path is wise thought or intention. The first stanzas of the Dhammapada, one of the most popular and beloved of Buddha's teachings, begin like this:

> *Mind is the forerunner of all states. Mind is Chief, King or Queen. If a person thinks or acts from a mind rooted in greed, hatred or ill-will then suffering follows them like the wheel in the track of the ox.*
>
> *Mind is the forerunner of all states. Mind is Chief, King or Queen. If a person thinks or acts from a mind rooted in wisdom, harmlessness and goodwill, then happiness follows them like the moon in the path of the stars.*

Wise intention is a way of clarifying the kind of person you want to be and how you want to act in the world.

This does not mean you never have feelings of greed, irritation, anger or hatred. Nor does it mean you never have a desire to cause harm. It means that you are aware of these thoughts and feelings when they arise and you do not act on them. In this way, you weaken the intention to do harm.

When you feel different forms of greed arising—like desire, lust or wishing things to be different than they are—then you can choose to restrain them and to be content or generous instead. When ill will arises in its various forms—anger, hostility, fear, anxiety or irritation, for example—then you set the intention of goodwill. When the impulse to be cruel arises in its various forms—aggression, destruction, suppressing or shaming—then turn your mind toward love, compassion and harmlessness.

Turning your intention toward goodwill or harmlessness does not mean that you ignore or suppress your feelings. It means that you allow those feelings to be what they are and treat yourself with goodwill and kindness.

The Roles of Renunciation, Patience and Goodwill in Wise Intention

Renunciation is not a popular practice in our time. We are taught to go for whatever we want with the belief that we will then be satisfied. This is a central tenet of consumerism. In working with renunciation, we practice being aware of the desire to acquire. We observe the clinging nature or heat of desire. We watch the stories the mind spins about how wonderful it will be to fulfill some desire. In some instances, when no harm will ensue, we allow ourselves to act on the desires. A desire for a treat after a healthy meal, a massage or other form of self-care, seeds or plants for the garden, flowers for the kitchen or equipment necessary to work can all be desires fulfilled without harming ourselves. In others, we restrain ourselves and let go of the desire to have or possess. When we desire sweets instead of healthy foods, alcohol or drugs as compensation for a hard day or shopping to salve a hurt, we can harm ourselves by fulfilling desires. In positive terms, renunciation is the practice of being content with what we have.

While renunciation includes consideration of the impacts of fulfilling a desire on others and the environment, it should not be taken to mean one should never fulfill a desire when it causes any kind of harm. If taken to an unhealthy extreme, one can become paralyzed, hopeless, cynical or guilt-ridden by an excessive assumption of personal responsibility for an unsustainable system. This would be an unwise application of renunciation.

It is difficult to learn renunciation when feelings of desire are strong. It is better to begin to practice renunciation when you are feeling calm and content. Then, set your intention to be attentive and not give in to every desire. Later, when you find yourself full of desire, longing or greed, again, set your intention toward restraint. Observe carefully how it feels to restrain your desire.

Another way to practice renunciation is to pause before acquiring something and ask yourself two questions:

- Do I really want this?

- Will it be good for me and others?

Over time, as you follow the Eightfold Path, these two questions will arise naturally and guide you in acting on your desires.

Patience is another attribute of wise intention. Patience is born from mindfully suffering impatience. We explored this in Chapter 4, with the hindrance of desire and imagining you have a desire for a cookie or to check your texts while meditating. Another way to mindfully transform impatience occurs when you are waiting for something. The next time you are caught in traffic or are in the slow line at the grocery store you teach yourself how to be patient. Observe the discomfort and sense of urgency in your body. Notice the thoughts about yourself and others that arise. Look out for anger and irritability or hatred. Remember that you have made the intention to become a patient person. You might practice mindfulness of breathing. Realizing that the people around you are probably also suffering you might add a lovingkindness mantra to your attention to the sensations of breathing. On the inbreath say silently, *May I be patient and free from suffering.* On the outbreath repeat, *May all these people be patient and free from suffering.* Remember that becoming a patient person is a lifetime project, so be gentle with yourself.

Like renunciation and patience, goodwill is an attribute of wise intention. Goodwill is being friendly, loving and kind to people, even when you are experiencing irritation, or you just don't like them. You can also practice goodwill toward yourself by replacing the negative and shaming things you say to yourself with positive words.

Sometimes, certain people or situations in your life repeatedly give rise to feelings like anger or guilt. You can tell if someone plays that role in your life because when you are in their company, a pattern of strong negative feelings arises. While practicing wise intention means that you set an intention to not behave badly, it does not mean that you allow yourself to be treated poorly. Just as you can practice wise intention by replacing negative things you say to yourself with positive ones, you can also practice it by not subjecting yourself to situations that repeatedly elicit negative feelings and thoughts.

Let's return to the credit card story. When I was in the midst of a storm of negative feelings, renunciation and restraint served me very well. The mental storm was my problem. It was my mind's response to the situation involving the bank. The fact that the credit card was not working was the bank's responsibility. The fact that I had a storm of feelings was my responsibility. The bank did not create my feelings. The bank just messed up. It is the same in every situation. We are responsible for our reactions to oue experiences and our reactions to our feelings.

Each one of us is responsible for our own reactivity. You can set an intention to not be the kind of person who fosters and supports angry storms. With that intention, you can set the intention to be loving and do no harm. When you fulfill your intention, you end up feeling good that you did not leave behind a trail of wreckage. Over time and with practice, you will find you manage both minor and major events that happen in your life with greater ease.

You can test whether the lessons of wise intention are true by asking yourself:

- What are my intentions?
- What do I aspire for in my actions?
- What happens when my intent is to be loving, wise, kind and to do no harm?
- What happens when it is otherwise?

Wise intention and wise view are the first two facets of the Eightfold Path. We learn them at the beginning of our journey, and they radically transform our worldview and how we behave in our lives. The rest of the path, including our behavior in the world and training the mind through meditation, is intended to test the truthfulness and accuracy of the wisdom that is presented right at the beginning. At first, this is an interesting hypothesis about life; it becomes in the end a realized truth.

A person is wise when their worldview is in keeping with the world as it is, meaning they see things as they really are. Seeing reality clearly, you will quite naturally be compassionate and loving.

Wise Speech on the Eightfold Path

The third facet of the Eightfold Path is wise speech. How we speak, including how we communicate in writing or online, can do great harm or remarkable good. The ability to communicate instantly anonymously or with avatars online through text, social media or comments can create the conditions that allow us to communicate in ways that are unwise. We can injure with our speech in ways that are every bit as real as injuring someone physically. The models that we are offered in the media and modern culture do not provide us very effective ways of speaking. The same problems existed in the time of the Buddha, and he provided fine guidance concerning speaking.

In order to do no harm with our speech, we use mindfulness to help us refrain from lying, slander, gossip and idle chatter. The last of these, idle chatter, pertains to meaningless speech that is used to avoid silence and simply being present. Most of what is heard in the media is idle chatter. Of course, some of what might be called idle chatter is necessary as social grease, when the content of what we are saying is not important but we are nonverbally reassuring each other of our caring, attention and goodwill.

There are five characteristics of speaking skillfully. They are truthfulness, helpfulness, necessity, kindness and timeliness.

When you can say yes to all the following questions, then you are speaking wisely:

- Is what I am about to say truthful?
- Is what I am about to say helpful?
- Is what I am about to say necessary?
- Is what I am about to say kind?
- Is this the right time to say it?

It is important to ask yourself whether the words you choose to say are truthful, helpful, necessary, kind and timely for you as well as for the other person. Something you want to say may be true and helpful, but not necessary. Try not saying it.

Similarly, you may have something to say that is necessary, but you are unable to say it kindly in that moment. Try waiting until you can speak out of kindness, and without rancor.

Sometimes, something you have to say may be truthful, helpful, necessary and kind, but it is not the right time for the statement to be uttered. Then it is wise to wait for the right time to speak. Other times, we may seek to protect someone by not saying anything, and in doing so, harm ourselves. Sometimes, in the end, we harm our relationship and the other person by waiting too long to speak. In such a circumstance, it is wise and skillful to speak.

Wise speech does not mean avoiding difficult conversations. Nor does it mean that every time you speak, great peace, beauty and love will be the result. As you develop your skills in wise speech, you will negotiate difficult conversations with greater wisdom. After a difficult encounter, you will experience greater ease from your part in the exchange.

Wise speech also does not mean that you never express anger or other difficult emotions. It does not mean that you should suppress those difficult feelings. Suppressing feelings is a form of violence against yourself. The suppressed feelings do not go away; they just come out sideways and in unexpected moments. Sometimes this indirect expression of emotions is especially apparent in people who will only permit themselves to say nice things.

Wise speech *does* mean that when you express difficult feelings, you do so in a way that minimizes harm. For example, you might bring up difficult feelings with a friend or therapist who is not involved in the situation that gave rise to the feelings. Exploring your feelings in this type of environment is wise because the other person is one who can listen without judgment or reactivity.

Wise Action on the Eightfold Path

The fourth facet of the Eightfold Path is wise or skillful action. When you act wisely your actions do no harm and are of benefit to yourself and others. You are in harmony with life and your actions lead to love, connection and happiness.

Every spiritual tradition has a moral and ethical code that provides guidance for your behavior. In the Buddhist tradition this guidance is offered through guidelines known as the Five Precepts. These will be explained much more thoroughly in the next chapter. Living according to the Precepts is a journey and an intentional practice. By being mindful of the impacts our actions have on ourselves and others, we learn how unwise action leads to unhappiness. It's hard to be happy when you are doing things that harm yourself or others. If you think about the unskillful things you have done in the past, you may have feelings of shame, guilt, anger or confusion. You probably keep these parts of your life hidden from other people. Hiding who you are sends a message to yourself that you are not worthy.

If you are doing something you know is not good for you, try stopping, even if for just a day or a week. If you have always wanted to do something that is good for you, start doing it and see how it makes you feel. You will find that there is a deep happiness that comes from living morally and ethically.

Enjoy this. Changing habits is hard at first, but over time, you will come to see that living a moral and ethical life gives you contentment and happiness. This is sometimes called *uprightness of heart.*

Wise Livelihood on the Eightfold Path

The fifth facet of the Eightfold Path is wise livelihood. Wise livelihood is doing work that causes no harm. It is work that contributes to the well-being of yourself, others and the planet. Being of service is one way to think about wise livelihood.

Work that takes vitality and joy away from you or others is not wise. Nor is work that requires you to manipulate others or that does not allow you to be completely honest. Any livelihood that encourages greed, hatred or ignorance is not wise.

A test for wise livelihood is to ask whether the work you are doing is harming yourself, other people or the planet. As you practice mindfulness, over time you will become more attuned to what skillful work is, and eventually you will be unable to engage in unwise work.

One of my students worked as a manager at a sales company. She had been listening to my dharma talks at Portland Insight Meditation Community for several months when she realized she had to quit her job. The sales quotas her boss put on the people she managed kept getting higher and higher. Her job was to enforce these goals, and to fire people if they did not meet them. She was required to treat people in harsh and unkind ways that caused a lot of conflict. She reached a point when she could not do it anymore.

Another one of my students was an executive in a tech company and made a large salary. As he practiced more, it became increasingly obvious to him that his boss created a culture of fear and panic. He considered if there was any way to intervene and realized he was powerless to do so. He could not be a part of it anymore and quit. For each of these people, leaving their jobs was a big step, and a huge risk financially.

A third student worked for a manufacturing company that created very precise parts for medical devices as well as parts for guided missiles. He discovered that he could no longer allow his work to contribute to the manufacture of weapons. He considered quitting, but in the end he negotiated with his boss to work only on the part of the business that produced medical equipment, enabling him to keep his job and follow the Eightfold Path.

Sometimes life circumstances might not allow you to quit a job that you know is at odds with your moral aspirations. This poses a potent dilemma. If you must stay, you can still do your best to practice your path of awakening and especially lovingkindness and compassion toward yourself and the people you work with.

Wise action, wise speech and wise livelihood concern our everyday behavior. Our actions and behavior in life are wise when we do no harm and bolster our own happiness and the happiness of others.

Wise Effort on the Eightfold Path

The last three facets of the Eightfold Path concern meditation and the training of mind.

A useful way to imagine wise effort is to liken the mind to a garden. In gardening we choose a spot with the correct amount of sun for a desired crop. We clear the land, plant the seeds for our crop and then provide it with rain, compost and manure. We remove weeds whenever they arise and do our best to keep them from returning. In the garden of the mind, we are seeking a rich crop of mindfulness, concentration, joy, compassion, love, generosity and equanimity.

To cultivate our mental garden, we make the effort to restrain undesired or unwholesome mental states. The second effort is to maintain their absence once the undesired mental states are gone. The third effort is to bring wholesome states into being and the fourth is to maintain and develop them once they are present.

Unwholesome states have their origins in greed, hatred and ignorance. Wholesome states, meanwhile, arise from generosity, love, compassion and wisdom, and the primary wholesome state is rooted in mindfulness and concentration.

The Effort To Restrain Unwholesome States

The first wise effort is to restrain unwholesome mental states. Restraint is not a popular idea, but it can be very helpful in navigating the difficulties of today's world, alleviating suffering and finding happiness. When an unwholesome state arises, try to restrain it.

In the credit card story, unwholesome mental states arose for me over and over through the day. I watched the storms rage. They were autonomous. But though they arose by themselves, I was aware of their coming and going. With a little less awareness, I could have gone into the cycle of *These damn banks, how come none of the top guys are going to jail with the crash they caused and profited from?* I could have created a whole series of storms inside. But I noticed the arising of the storms of anger and irritation and allowed them to pass without getting riled up or acting out.

By noticing the arising of agitated thoughts and feelings, I could practice restraint. Over the day, unwholesome states of anger arose again and again. I would notice the arising of anger and I would interrupt it by returning my attention to the breath. Anger would arise again, and I would turn my attention to the thoughts and feelings. I would notice them arise, then dissipate, then disappear and then notice what arose next. All of these were ways to restrain an unwholesome state once it had arisen.

In your own life, think back to a time when you told yourself stories about how you had been wronged or why something should have been different. Notice that when the story is happening, you are consumed by thoughts and feelings characterized by *I, I, me, me, mine, mine.* You can recognize an *I, I, me, me, mine, mine* storm by the intensity of the desire for things to be different from the way they are, coupled with a miasma of difficult feelings and thoughts. In one of these storms, it might feel like you are seeing things with perfect clarity, but that clarity is fed by intense emotions. When you notice the *I, I, me, me, mine, mine* storm, try not to feed it. Just observe the chorus of *I, I, me, me, mine, mine* without judgment and with kindness toward yourself.

As noted earlier, mental states rooted in greed, hatred, anger or ignorance are unwholesome. However, the teachings of the Eightfold Path do not say you should never feel hatred, anger or greed. It does not mean you are a bad person if you have these feelings. In the teachings on the Eightfold Path, there is no edict that says, "Never feel anger, hatred or greed." During my credit card storm, thoughts of, *You're bad, you shouldn't get angry,* did not come up. Instead, the thoughts that came were, *Wow, these seeds of unwholesome states are still in here and in the right circumstances they can spring up and a very unpleasant painful mental state can bloom.*

While it is important to experience all your feelings, it is equally important to understand that you can choose which thoughts and feelings to cultivate.

Early in my career I was teaching meditation at a drug and alcohol treatment center. My audience was a room full of doctors and nurses, all addicts. At the end, after everybody left, one of the women doctors returned up the stairs with tears in her eyes. She said, *Are you saying I can choose not to follow certain thoughts or feelings?* After I told her that was indeed a choice she could make, she stood sobbing before me. *It had never occurred to me,* she said.

Sometimes, we might indulge in rage, mistaking our painful and unpleasant feelings of hatred as pleasant, or feelings of self-righteousness as virtue. Because of this confusion, we might choose to cultivate anger, hatred, greed or ignorance. This is partly because the storm of feelings releases biochemical stimulants, norepinephrine and adrenaline, that are central to the fight-flight-freeze response. It can be very difficult to practice wise effort when in the midst of an *I, I, me, me, mine, mine* biochemical storm.

How then to move forward? Practicing restraint in less challenging situations develops your skills for the storms. So, start small. The next time you want yet another cookie or the next time feelings of mild irritation at a loved one arise, use the opportunity to practice restraint of the unwholesome state. Do not eat the cookie. Sit with the feelings and thoughts that come up. Or if you eat the cookie, do so very mindfully, paying attention to every detail in the moment as much as you can. Each time you do this, you develop your capacity for wise effort.

When the tumult is happening and there is enough mindfulness, why not restrain it? Come back to the breath or go for a walk. Do something that does not feed that storm. This is the effort to restrain unwholesome states.

Sometimes the same angry, hateful or other difficult thoughts or feelings come up over and over. In these cases, it might not be wise to practice restraint. If you have noticed a pattern of difficult thoughts or feelings arising, the next time you experience it, you might experiment with letting it play out. Go to a safe space, perhaps your meditation seat. Take the thoughts or feelings as your meditation object. Notice every aspect of the storm. Attend to it with great curiosity. There might be some part of your psychology or past that needs to process the thoughts or feelings in the light of your loving, mindful attention.

We all have relapses and act out old patterns. My credit card storm was a relapse. Relapse is an important phenomenon. People tend to think, *Oh no, I relapsed,* and castigate themselves, but relapses are very educational. They mean there was something to learn. Failure presents a golden opportunity to better understand the workings of the mind. It also helps with arrogance. For me, the credit card storm dispelled some conceit that I am beyond irritation and anger.

The Effort To Maintain the Absence of Unwholesome States

Once an unwholesome state is restrained, wise effort would be to keep it restrained. When the angry, hateful, greedy or ignorant thoughts come up again, nip them in the bud. You can try telling those thoughts, *No thanks, I don't need this thought right now.* And when the thoughts come back again, pay very close attention to the details of the breath. Pay particular attention to the moments of the beginning and ending of each breath. This is the effort to restrain the unwholesome states. The effort to restrain unwholesome states is not denial. It is not detaching from difficult feelings and pretending you never have them. The effort to restrain unwholesome states includes being very mindful of the state arising or soon after it has arisen as well as bringing the mind back to focus on the breath or chosen meditation object.

The wise effort of maintaining the absence of unwholesome states does not mean you should not process grief or past traumas. That would be using the principle of wise effort in a repressive and unskillful way. Processing grief means you encounter difficult feelings like anger, despair and sadness. Sometimes, it is necessary to get help from someone, like a friend or therapist, who is not involved in the circumstances that gave rise to the trauma. Most people at some time need support to process aspects of their psychology or past.

Guarding the Sense Doors

Unskillful behaviors often arise from dwelling or obsessing on unwholesome thoughts or intentions. The more time you spend thinking about something that is unwholesome, the more likely you are to act on those thoughts. Wise restraint would be to draw the mind away from those thoughts and intentions.

There is a practice for the wise effort of maintaining the absence of unwholesome states called guarding the sense doors. The sense doors are the eye, ear, nose, tongue, body and mind. When you are guarding the sense doors, your intent is to be aware of any sight, sound, smell, taste, feeling or thought in the moment that it arises, before it turns into concepts, interpretations and meanings. By acutely noticing what is happening at the sense doors, unwholesome states may not be able to gain much momentum. With this kind of directed attention, you can see things as they really are. Thoughts, feelings and sensations may arise, a storm may occur, but there is no attachment to or identification with any of it.

What does such a process look like in day-to-day existence? If you are meditating, you turn your mind back to your meditation object. If you are not meditating, you notice a feeling, impulse or thought arise, and determine whether it is something you wish to encourage. If it is unwholesome, then it can be relinquished. For an unwholesome thought or feeling, you can tell the thought or feeling, *No thank you,* and bring your mind back to the present. For other unwholesome sensory experiences, like consuming a food, intoxicant or other substance that is unhealthy but tempting, you can turn your attention to the unhealthy and unwholesome outcomes of imbibing. Each time you feel it draw you, turn your attention with greater detail to the unwholesomeness that is a result of indulging.

The Effort To Bring Wholesome States into Being

The most important wholesome states to cultivate are mindfulness and concentration. Developing these creates a sense of clarity and power that quite naturally brings all other wholesome states into being. Along with mindfulness and concentration come patience, tranquility, generosity and equanimity. It is like turning on the lights. Without the light, you are stumbling in the dark. The primary practice for the cultivation of wholesome capacities begins with paying attention to the breath. We use mindfulness of in and out breathing to develop the clarity to observe everything else that happens in the body and mind.

When I was a merchant marine, in my twenties, I liked spending time on the bridge of the ships I sailed on. I would watch as the direction of the 600-foot-long ship (as long as two football fields) danced back and forth in the waves. We were traversing the South Indian Ocean, and in a storm, sixty-foot waves tossed the ship so violently that it went nose down into a wave, then back up again.

On the bridge was a beautiful glowing gyrocompass that was mounted on gimbals so that it always stayed level. The captain used dials to set the specific direction he wanted the ship to travel. The waves pushed us off course one way or another, but the gyrocompass was connected to the rudder and corrected the direction as needed.

In mindfulness of breathing, our intended direction is to stay focused on the breath, each breath in and out. Because we have this conscious intention to focus on the breath, it becomes obvious when we are going off course. Mindfulness is the mysterious mental capacity to be aware of the wandering of the mind. It illuminates what the mind is doing.

Maybe today you sat and meditated for the first time in your life. Maybe you have been meditating for years. You may have sat for just a minute or thirty seconds. You may have sat for an hour or forty minutes today. Or maybe you sat for five minutes here and fifteen minutes there. Regardless of the duration, your practice is important. You become more and more aware of your resistance to accepting things as they are. You cultivate a desire to end suffering in yourself.

In the effort to cultivate, nurture and develop wholesomeness, we start with small things. We deal with bigger things over time. We gradually transform ourselves. We become much more loving and kind.

The effort to maintain and develop wholesome mental states is grounded in the last two facets of the Eightfold Path: wise mindfulness and wise concentration.

Wise Mindfulness on the Eightfold Path

The seventh facet of the Eightfold Path is wise mindfulness. Wise mindfulness is remembering to be awake to what is happening inside and around you in each moment. In order to be systematic and totally inclusive in examining the human experience, Buddha articulated four major categories to which we can attend. They are commonly called the four foundations of mindfulness. In the classical Buddhist texts these are referred to as *gocharas,* or pastures of abiding.

These pastures in which we are invited to abide are the body, feelings, mental formations and mental phenomena.

Body

Mindfulness of breathing is the most common starting point for mindfulness of the body practice. Our lives begin at birth with a gasping in breath and end with a final out breath. Between these two inevitable moments there is an unbroken rhythm of breathing in and breathing out. This breathing connects us intimately with all of life. The trees need our waste gasses and we need the oxygen they release. We are all part of one living and interconnected process.

Mostly the body breathes all by itself with no awareness. However, we can add mindfulness to this essential body function. We use the sensation of breathing, which exists only in the present moment, as an anchor to help us stay awake in the present. With the intention of staying present here and now with the breath, we notice more accurately when the mind wanders. Each breath becomes an invitation to be awake and aware and alive in the body rather than lost in the trance states of past and future.

Beyond mindfulness of breathing, we can systematically explore the nature of our experience of the body. How do you know you have a body? Right now, you can feel the chair in which you are sitting. Maybe there is a sensation in your belly or maybe your shoulders are hurting. Practicing in the pasture of the body means you focus awareness on your body.

In addition to the practice of mindfulness when sitting and breathing you can also practice a systematic walking meditation. Find a spot to walk back and forth and pay attention to the lifting, moving and placing of each foot. Come back again and again from the trances of the wandering mind. Walking meditation can be done any time you are moving from one place to another. It can morph into the mindfulness of paying attention to your body when you exercise, walk to the car, chop wood or wash the dishes.

Another strategy of body awareness is to attend carefully to each body part. This is called body scanning. Take a moment to notice how your feet feel, just noting how you know you have feet. Do they feel tired? Itchy? Relaxed? Is there no feeling at all? Notice this and move on to the ankles, calves, thighs, hips, the pelvic region, the belly, the chest, the expanse of the back, shoulders, arms, hands. Notice the life in your face. Notice your mouth, cheeks, the area around your eyes, ears, forehead. Notice the top of your head.

You can practice mindfulness of the body when you are waiting in line, sitting in the car, on the phone or lying in bed unable to sleep.

You can use mindfulness of the body to bring more of your life into the realm of mindfulness. Observe yourself getting out of bed, brushing your teeth, showering, dressing, changing the baby's diaper, chopping carrots, driving the car and every other activity of your day. Become curious just how much of your life you can notice mindfully.

When you are sick you have the perfect opportunity to meditate. Sickness has unpleasant symptoms: sore throat, pain, fever, nausea . . . these are all integral aspects of life in a human body. Don't miss the chance to be present when you are sick.

Wherever you are and whatever you are doing, it is possible to become mindful and plop into the body.

Feelings

The second foundation of mindfulness is attention to feelings. The use of the word *feelings* in this context is rather precise and should not be confused with emotions which we also refer to as feelings. Feelings in this context can be pleasant, unpleasant or not yet decided. They arise when our senses come into contact with their respective sense objects. There are pleasant sights, sounds, smells, tastes, touches and thoughts. Likewise, there are unpleasant experiences at each sense door. Many experiences have a neutral or not yet decided valence or weighting.

Feelings drive us through life. We hunger for and seek pleasant feelings and reject and avoid the unpleasant. We tend to go into a state of ignorance, denial or lack of awareness in response to neutral feelings. When mindfulness of feeling is present, we can choose to endure some unpleasant feelings or not chase after some pleasant ones. We develop some spiritual maturity and are no longer at the whim of every feeling that comes along.

Feelings manifest in the body. Take a moment now to tune into the feelings in your body. Where do you feel them? Are the feelings pleasant, unpleasant or neutral?

Practicing in this pasture means noticing as a feeling arises, and then noticing as it passes and disappears. The next time you become aware of having a feeling, take some time and try to notice every detail of it. Notice where it lives in your body. Ask yourself how you know you are feeling that feeling. Try to stay aware of the feeling from the moment you notice it until the moment it passes away. Once it has passed, see if you can notice when the next feeling begins to arise. When thoughts about the feeling start, notice them and then bring your awareness back to how you are feeling. Try to stay with whatever feeling comes up until it passes.

Mind and Mental Formations

The mind and its contents become the realm of observation in the third foundation of mindfulness. We observe the thoughts and emotions that arise. We take our personality patterns, moods and the stories that the mind tells as objects rather than identifying with them as self. We observe if the mind is expansive or contracted. We notice whether the thoughts and emotions that are present are rooted in wisdom, love and compassion or whether they are driven by greed, hatred or ignorance. Practicing mindfulness of the mind and mental formations, we disidentify with the contents of the mind as they arise and disappear. Observing the mind in this way allows us to intervene when experiences like fear and self-hatred arise. It also allows us to recognize when desirable states of mind are present so we can reinforce them.

Mental Phenomena

The last of the four realms to explore with mindfulness is mental phenomena. This opens our perception to the basic building blocks of our experience. We learn to perceive the existential reality of the Four Noble Truths.

We can attend mindfully to the presence or absence of the five hindrances: desire, aversion, restlessness and agitation, sloth and torpor, and doubt.

We become aware of the seven enlightenment factors, which makes it possible to cultivate them. They are mindfulness, curiosity, persistence, joy, concentration, tranquility and equanimity.

Huge vistas of practice open when we realize that we can actively observe the real-time operation of the sense doors. It is fascinating to observe seeing, smelling, hearing, tasting, touching and thinking as phenomena as they arise and disappear.

As mindfulness and concentration develop, you will notice that all phenomena arise and pass away spontaneously. You will notice that the liking and disliking of phenomena, and even the noticing itself also arise and pass away spontaneously.

The four foundations of mindfulness contain all our experience as human beings. There is nothing left out. All the experiences we identify as *I, me and mine* are revealed to be impersonal. They are seen to be impermanent, unsatisfactory and to not contain an enduring self. What began as a hypothetical map of consciousness at the beginning of the journey is realized as consisting of indisputable facts. This is the path of true happiness revealing itself.

Wise Concentration on the Eightfold Path

Concentration is the ability of the mind to focus on one thing and stay there. Everyone has some capacity to concentrate. It is strengthened by school, playing a sport or learning to play an instrument. Meditation, in which the mind is returned countless times to a chosen object of attention, results in a high level of concentration. Every time you return awareness to the experience of the arising and passing of the breath you are strengthening concentration. When you move beyond superficial awareness of the sensations of breathing and engage more intimately with the actual sensations, you are further strengthening concentration.

One way to envision concentration is to imagine it as coming upon a hammock on a beautiful sunny day. You climb into the hammock and simply rest there without straying, in perfect ease. You are not trying to achieve anything other than being present at rest in the hammock. Climb into the sensations of breathing, into the present moment and rest there.

You can experience concentration right now. Bring awareness to your chest and abdomen and take one nice deep breath while paying attention. That is concentration. You just did it. You had a moment of a concentrated mind. It happens one moment at a time, so you can enjoy each moment of concentration you have. You may notice that when awareness is concentrated on the sensations of breathing, thoughts and other disturbances cease to exist. This is one of the great pleasures of meditation practice. You get to take a break.

One of the skills that is developed through meditation is knowing how much effort to exert in keeping the mind on its chosen meditation object. There are many ways to strengthen concentration. It helps to be clear in your intention when you sit down to meditate. If you are planning to do mindfulness of breathing, be clear about that. Know where you are planning to anchor your attention, with the sensations in the chest and abdomen or at the nostrils. If you are working specifically to strengthen concentration, know that you will return diligently to the breath. To further strengthen concentration, you might add a repetitive phrase or mantra. On the inbreath silently say, *May I be happy*, on the outbreath say, *May all beings be happy*. You could further support concentration by adding the use of a mala or prayer beads. At the end of each cycle of the breath mindfully slide a bead between your fingers.

Concentration and mindfulness work together to allow us to really observe and understand what is occurring. If you want to chop down a tree, it is essential to have an axe that is both sharp and heavy. Either characteristic without the other won't work. Concentration, with its capacity for focus is akin to the heaviness. Mindfulness with its capacity of penetration is the sharpness.

Exploring the Territory of the Eightfold Path

This chapter gave you a map of the Eightfold Path. I hope that you will have enough familiarity with it to begin a lifelong journey of exploring the territory it describes. The more you learn about the path and yourself the more interesting the path will become.

Over the course of forty years, the Buddha refined the teachings to help a myriad of people with different psychological states to realize that freedom lies within the human mind. He helped people see that happiness and freedom do not come from beauty, consumption, wealth or status, self-denial or deprivation. Happiness and freedom come from developing one's own mind and realizing that you have profound responsibility for what happens in your consciousness and behavior.

Storm Watch Exercise

The first time I had a conscious emotional storm I was about 23 years old. I had finished my first ten-day retreat with Satya Narayan Goenka, in India in 1971. (Goenka was authorized to teach by U Ba Khin, who also authorized my teacher Ruth Denison.) My girlfriend and I were on a year-long overland journey from Europe to India. We were in the town of Goa, a lovely beach town.

I was unable to tolerate conflict at that time in my life, and we had just had one of our non-fights. We would not argue with words, but it would be clear to anyone observing us that we were not getting along. I was feeling awful and confused and left to go walk in the night. It was a full moon, and as I walked something happened that I had never noticed before—an inner storm arose. I did not know what it was. I had never had the capacity to be aware of my own anger. It was rage. I walked all night, watching the inner storm rage. It was my first experience of consciously noticing a mental storm. By dawn, it was gone.

Look back at a time when you were very angry. Try to find a time when you remember lots of details. Focus on what happened in you that was not words or thoughts, but in the body. Was there anger in your body? How did you know you were angry? Was there fear? How did you know there was fear? Did you check out? Where was the experience in your body?

Now, the next time you feel the slightest twinge of anger, fear or numbness, try stepping away from the situation if you can. Tell the other person you will call them back as soon as you can or tell the person in the room you must leave but you will be back soon. If possible, write down every thought and feeling as it comes up. If you cannot write them down, note each one by saying out loud to yourself, *I notice that I am feeling* . . . (and say your feeling). Sometimes you will have complete thoughts; sometimes it will be just a half sentence or words combined with garbled feelings. Just note this. Notice also where the anger, fear or numbness is in your body. Note how your breathing is, how your heart is beating, the posture of your body, how your jaw is set. Stay with the feeling if you can. If you are unable to stay with the feeling and instead find yourself acting on it, then notice this.

First Arrow Exercise

Buddha taught there are everyday forms of suffering that we all experience. These experiences of suffering hold through time and across cultures. Let's revisit them: [BL1–4]

- Being with people you do not want to be with;
- Not being with the people you want to be with;
- Having experiences you do not want to have;
- Not having experiences you want to have.

Take a moment right now to scan where you're experiencing suffering. Is there someone your heart longs for who is gone or someone you hoped and imagined would be in your life but who never appeared? Is there someone you wish you had never met or would never see again? Does your body hurt, or do you have an illness? Is there something in your life you feel is missing? Do you have a sense of loss? Are you lonely or depressed?

Once you have compiled your inventory of suffering, imagine that your beloved child, pet or someone else whom you dearly adore was suffering in the same way. What would you say to acknowledge their suffering? What would you say or do to comfort them? Comfort yourself with these loving, kind and generous words and thoughts.

6

The Five Precepts

Guides to Happiness

So far today, I have done all right.
I haven't gossiped.
I haven't lost my temper.
I haven't been greedy or grumpy, nasty or self-centered.
I am really glad of that.
But, in a few minutes,
I am going to get out of bed,
and then I am going to need a lot of help.

—POPULAR SAYING

WE ARE PREDISPOSED TO being fearful, angry, greedy and sexually impulsive. Our first impulse when we encounter another being is to ask, *Do I have to fight it?* Our next impulse, assuming we feel safe, is to ask, *Can I eat it?* Following that, the impulse that comes up is, *Can I mate with it?*

Safety, eating and mating are basic survival instincts. We share these three primary impulses with every other animal on earth. When we were still living in caves, or in the grasslands of the savannah, our survival impulses served us well. They allowed us to go to battle instantly and defend ourselves when suddenly attacked. Without our survival impulses, we would have perished as a species. But unchecked, they can drive us to great harm.

As humans, we have found ways to manage our primary impulses so that we can live together in relative harmony. Over the course of our evolution, we discovered how to get along with each other on a societal scale and on a personal level. We developed behavioral norms and systems to enforce our norms. We established different types of systems: economic systems, governmental systems, legal systems and ethical systems. Religions are yet another kind of system.

Today, the dominant religions on our planet are Judaism, Christianity, Hinduism, Taoism, Islam and Buddhism. One thing they have in common is a set of moral and ethical guidelines or rules. These religious traditions have different terms for the concept of precepts, but they each have a code of behavior that serves the common purpose of helping us live together peacefully. When we follow these precepts, and live with integrity to our highest aspirations, we experience what the Buddha called *uprightness of heart*. This is a deep inner ease that allows us to feel at home with ourselves, our community and the world.

The Five Precepts

In Buddhism, there are five precepts or guidelines that help us to be loving and at ease.

The five precepts are:

1. I undertake the training of the heart to refrain from taking the life of another being.

2. I undertake the training of the heart to refrain from taking what is not freely given.

3. I undertake the training of the heart to refrain from sexual acts that cause harm.

4. I undertake the training of the heart to refrain from harmful speech.

5. I undertake the training of the heart to refrain from using intoxicants.

We will explore each precept from two perspectives: First, we will approach them through the traditional interpretation of the precepts based on restraint. Second, we will investigate them through a positive articulation of the precepts that encourages the cultivation of skillful behavior. Over the course of my teaching the Dharma, I have translated the precepts into this positive perspective because it helps us shape our behavior in ways that lead to happiness.

As you adopt the precepts in your daily life, you will experience a growing sense of ease in your mindfulness practice. You will observe that when your actions are not in accord with the precepts, there is greater restlessness, worry, aversion, desire or doubt when you meditate. You may also find you have more problems with insomnia or bad moods. When there is less uproar in our lives, it is reflected in greater tranquility internally. Over time, this sense of ease will seep into your everyday life and following the precepts will become more natural.

It is helpful to think of the precepts as natural laws, like the laws of physics or chemistry. Just as we know that an object with mass will fall to the ground if released while close to the planet, so we can predict that when we act in ways that harm ourselves or others, suffering will ensue. Understood like this, the precepts become consciousness-raising reminders. Like applying our understanding of scientific laws to explain observed physical phenomena, when we find ourselves suffering as a result of some action, we can look back and see if following the precepts might have prevented the painful outcome.

The precepts are not intended to be vehicles for guilt trips or a basis for perfectionist expectations. We are humans and quite capable of deluded, greedy or hateful behavior. Each precept is a practice. Therefore, each one begins with the phrase *I undertake the training of the heart.*

Traditional Precept 1: Do No Harm

The traditional translation of the first precept is, *I undertake the training of the heart to refrain from taking the life of another being.*

One of the functions of the precepts is to raise your consciousness about your actions. Using the first precept this way can be very helpful. This understanding guides you to think about the genesis of your actions and become aware of impulses inside you. There are three questions you can ask yourself to help reveal your impulses. They are:

- What are the ways I harm others or myself through my impulse of violence?

- What are ways I harm others or myself through my impulses that arise from fear, anger, greed or jealousy?

- What are ways I harm others or myself through my other primal and basic impulses?

Instead of trying to deny that you have such impulses, you can under-stand that as a human you were born with them. With this understanding, you can develop your ability to live with awareness of the arising of your pri-mary impulses. As you practice mindfulness, you will be more able to notice when primitive impulses arise. Instead of acting on impulse, you watch the storm of feelings and thoughts. With awareness of their arising, intensifying, abating and passing, you are more prepared to act in ways that do no harm.

In its most stark and important form the first precept says that we are not to kill another human. Over the course of human history, we have prov-en time and time again that we are remarkably capable of killing each other. In almost every country on this planet, we take ordinary young men and women and put them through a dehumanization training. We train them to point weapons, pull the trigger and kill other people. Right now, human beings are killing other humans. Imagine if our government adopted this precept. Imagine how many schools, hospitals, and parks we could build if we no longer put our resources into ways to kill other people.

The first precept guides us to live as harmlessly as we can. We cannot live a life that does not result in the death of other beings. When you dig in the garden, drive your car or burn wood in the fireplace to keep warm, your actions result in the death of many creatures. Even as a vegetarian or vegan the production of your food involves much death. When you bring your food to your plate, walk along the pavement from the front door to the grocery store, or take antibiotics, you are killing thousands of small creatures from germs to bugs. Life lives on life. Even the Buddha instructed his monks to eat what they were offered and to refuse meat only if it had been killed specifi-cally for them. This precept means that when you do something that involves the death of another being, don't do it wantonly or unconsciously.

The Story of Ratty

A while ago, a rat ventured into our home. We could hear it at night as it ran across the ceiling. The rat had access to the kitchen through the hole under the stove where the power and gas lines entered, and there were occasional rat droppings near the dog food.

I decided that we would coexist with the creature we named Ratty since he seemed to be doing us no harm. I knew there was a disease risk, but it seemed minor and I was intent upon following the precept of refraining from killing. There was no place to put a live trap other than right in the middle of our small kitchen.

My daughter Tara's bedroom was in the basement. One day she came running upstairs quite agitated. Ratty had run from behind a dresser and across her foot. I realized that Ratty had to go.

I agonized about how to do it. Every way of killing seemed awful. Traditional spring-loaded traps are gruesome. Poison is a torturous way to die. The poison makes the rat voraciously thirsty. It goes outside to find water and ideally doesn't return to die inside the walls, where it would create both a terrible stink and crop of large black flies. I investigated and found that there is a commercially available device called a Rat Zapper. It runs on three AA batteries that store up a large electrical charge in a capacitor. When the rat steps on a metal plate and touches its nose to the second pole where the food is, "zap," it's electrocuted and dies instantly.

I purchased the zapper, brought it home and placed it under the stove. The entire process felt yucky. I kept reflecting on the precept of abstaining from killing. I sat in meditation and investigated the feelings that this plan to kill Ratty brought up. The anticipation of killing was uncomfortable.

I reflected upon the Zen story of monks approaching the Roshi and asking him what to do when the Dharma Hall was overrun with fleas. His reply—"Well, kill them of course. With compassion."—provided little comfort.

It took a few days, but one morning when I checked the trap, I saw a long tail sticking out of it. My heart sank. I had killed a fellow being. I removed Ratty and placed him on a newspaper. This killing felt personal. There were cute little whiskers, a long pointy nose and a beautiful gray pelt. This not-so-small being was hardly different from the gerbils, hamsters and guinea pigs we had loved and cared for as pets when the children were small.

I sat with Ratty for a while and offered my apologies for having killed him. I explained my reasons, wished him well on his journey, chanted the Homage and Refuge chants and prayed that he be born as a human in his next life so that he could hear and practice the Dharma. Then I buried him out in the front yard, where a year before we had buried our beloved dog, Kali.

Just in case there was a second rat, I set the zapper again. Two days later there was another dead, fully grown rat. Again I sat with it, wished it a good rebirth and buried it in the front yard with a simple ceremony.

This happened five more times. Seven large rats had been living in our house!

I noticed that my distress diminished each time I found a rat in the trap. It seemed that I could get used to killing rats. I sat with this reality and realized how remarkably conditionable this human mind is.

Here we are, householders, living in the world. When our bodies are infected with bacteria, we kill them with antibiotics. We routinely use antibacterial soap and bleach and boiling water to kill bacteria and viruses. When our living cells mutate and become cancerous, we use surgery, radiation and chemotherapy to remove them. We also use a host of alternative treatments, including meditation and visualization, to strengthen the immune system so it can kill the cancer cells. Killing is part of the fabric of our lives.

The precept to abstain from killing provides priceless guidance as a consciousness-raising tool. It serves as a buffer against unconscious and wanton killing. The Dharma invites us to question, and to use our own wisdom to choose our actions. These intentional actions are karma and will have their *vipakka* (results).

What is the intention behind the action? Is it unwarranted or angry or hate-filled killing? Is this killing of rats motivated by compassion, lovingkindness and wisdom so that we don't have the risk of disease among our family? When I must, I will kill rats or mice. I do so with as much mindfulness, lovingkindness and compassion as possible. Taking a life requires of me the greatest respect, humility and reflection.

Rats live outside our house on the seeds that spill from our several bird feeders. I have a live trap with which I catch and release them in a forested park nearby. It pleases me to watch them scurry to freedom in the woods. I wish this could always be the outcome.

Positive Precept 1: Be Kind and of Service to All Beings

The positive interpretation of the first precept is:

I aspire to become kind and of service to all beings.

This precept encourages full engagement in life. With this perspective, you set your intention to be of service. When you combine this intention with mindfulness practice, over time you will find spontaneous feelings of love and compassion arising in your everyday life. Ways to be kind and of service will naturally arise.

Fully engaging in life with the intent to be of service does not mean that you never take a stand against something. It doesn't mean that you must be happy and positive about everything all the time. You will find that the more you become present, alive and aware of what is happening around you, the more likely you will be to take a stand when it is wise to do so. You will find you can no longer sit quietly by while others are harmed. You have a wider perspective and a deeper understanding of what is the wise and skillful thing to do. I have participated in nuclear weapons protests and peace marches. It took years of lovingkindness practice for me to understand that *those people* who are responsible for the proliferation of nuclear weapons are seeking to meet their safety needs. I imagine they feel they can never truly feel safe. I might act in the same way if the conditions were right. If someone was attacking my family, I would use all I had to defend my children, my partner and myself. Maybe this is how some people feel all the time. Today, I would still lay my life down to stop the detonation of a nuclear bomb, but I will not use physical violence in protest.

This precept also does not mean that you should suppress your basic impulses and urges. It does mean that you arrive at a place of complete acceptance of whatever arises within you, without judgment and with awareness of the impulse's arising. If you do not allow aspects of who you are to rise into consciousness, they do not just disappear. They stay inside you. The thoughts, imaginations, scenarios and experiences of anger, hatred, greed, fear or desire are suppressed and remain unconscious. Anything that exists within you that you cannot own is most likely projected onto others who you will perceive as bad, evil or otherwise worthy of being despised. Projecting is an ego defense which we use unconsciously to protect our self-image. You trick yourself into believing that something you can't tolerate as part of yourself exists outside of you. You can get a hint that you are projecting when you find yourself pointing your finger and saying, *They are the bad people* or *that is the evil empire.* With projection, you become incapable of seeing another person with compassion.

The first precept tells you that to act kindly and be of service you allow what actually exists to exist. You allow your own primal impulses to arise, and you do not act on them. You notice when you are speaking ill of another person. You do not judge yourself, but just notice and allow the next feeling to arise. Eventually, you come into greater awareness of the arising of the imaginations, scenarios or fantasies that are rooted in greed, hatred or delusion, as well as those that arise out of generosity, love and clarity. With this knowing, you develop your capacity for skillful choices and actions, and your ability to be kind and of service to all beings.

Traditional Precept 2: Not Taking What Is Not Freely Given

The traditional translation of the second precept is:

I undertake the training of the heart to refrain from taking what is not freely given.

This precept has far-reaching implications. Instead of decreeing specific actions, like larceny, shoplifting, tax evasion or blackmail as outside the law and allowing all other actions, the second precept guides you to become aware of the impact on your heart, body and mind from taking what *is* freely given and from taking something that *is not* freely given. It guides you to become aware of the reality of a situation in which you receive or take something. This can be tangible or intangible, a pen or a paycheck, a hug or someone's time. My teacher, Ruth Denison, used to say when teaching this precept, *Dahlink, once this practice gets under your skin, you can no longer get away with yourself.*

Many years ago, I had quite an awakening to this precept. I was working as a psychotherapist and one of my patients was a high-level executive at a bank. He was secretive about his personal information. He would not tell me anything about his family or disclose his contact information. He paid in cash after each session. Then one day he asked me for a receipt for all his payments. A chill ran through me. I had not been recording his sessions in my books. The thought arose, *Oh no, the IRS planted him.* For the rest of the day I felt great unease. The toll on the mind and body for cheating was much higher than any monetary gain. That night, when I got home, the first thing I did was record the missing income. What a relief. The cost to my integrity was vastly greater than the few dollars in saved taxes.

When you practice this precept, you will find that some things you have done in the past no longer feel right. You will find that it feels better not to take pens or Post-it pads from work anymore. You'll feel a sense of virtue from not taking two helpings of that delicious dish at a potluck before everyone else has had one helping. When the teller at the grocery store accidentally gives you extra cash, you will feel a surge of joy in your heart when you give it back. When you are in a conversation with someone and notice their body language closes up and it feels like you have to work harder to keep their attention, you will feel a sense of ease when you stop talking and ask them how they are feeling. Driving down the highway, when someone wants to merge, instead of cutting them off, you'll feel good about yourself for making room for them.

This precept applies to how you treat yourself as well. Most people deprive themselves of about two hours of sleep a day. In this way, we take from our body what is not freely given. When you practice this precept in relation to your body, you take a nap or go to sleep earlier so that your body gets enough sleep.

When you practice this precept, you might find yourself looking back on your past behavior. Perhaps you had a time in your life when you shoplifted, stole money from a friend or cheated on your taxes. It may have been a long time ago, or recently. It is easy to fall into a default sense of self-judgment and self-hatred if you do have such a past, but remember, the precept is to *undertake the training of the heart.* Instead of chastising yourself, be generous with yourself, and give yourself the time to sit with the circumstances that led you to take what was not freely given. If you can, talk about what was happening in your life at that time with a therapist or good friend. In some cases, it may become clear to you that making amends by returning what you took is the right thing to do. In other cases, finding other ways to give back, such as by helping others, practicing compassion or volunteering will feel like the right thing to do. Whatever you do, make reparations that will heal the wounds you have inflicted on your heart by taking what was not freely given. This precept should not be interpreted as calling for punishment. It should be used to guide you to a training of the heart that yields compassion and love for yourself and others.

Decades ago, during a retreat, a memory arose after many hours a day of meditation. I had stolen a salad when I was at college. I found myself emotionally struggling with it and the upset persisted off and on for several days of the retreat. With the help of my teacher, I resolved to go back to the cafeteria and pay for it the next time I could. A few months later I visited my old college town. When I gave the cafeteria manager the money and explained why, he looked at me oddly, but he accepted the payment. This act of restitution was quite comforting to me and re-established what the Buddhists speak of as uprightness of heart.

This precept should not be taken to mean that you do not deserve to receive anything. It should never be interpreted to mean that you are a burden on earth because your existence requires that you take from the earth for sustenance and in order to flourish. That way of thinking is grounded in a reverse sense of supremacy over mother nature because it denies the fact that you are part of the earth. Each being on this earth, a human as much as an ant, wolf or tree, is part of the earth and must take from the earth that which it needs to live.

The more you practice this precept, the better you feel about yourself.

Positive Precept 2: Be Generous

The positive interpretation of the second precept is:
I aspire to become generous to all beings.

This precept can be a lot of fun. When practicing generosity as a way of life, you will find all kinds of ways to be generous. The pleasure of sharing will become one of the great delights of your life.

Some fun and simple ways to practice this precept are to listen with great attentiveness to someone when they are talking. Meet another person's gaze with openness in your heart. Give and receive smiles whenever you can. Greet people with *Hello, how are you?* Give to yourself as well. When you go grocery shopping, buy yourself some flowers. Do something that feels like an indulgence but is good for you, like getting a massage or going on a retreat.

There are a myriad of little things you can do for others and yourself in everyday life to be generous. As you practice this precept, new ways to be generous will open up before you. Gradually, you will find there are times that your heart opens spontaneously. Eventually, you will notice that everywhere you turn there is ease. You will notice that the preciousness of life is awake in you.

This precept should not be taken to mean you should give at the expense of your well-being. With mindfulness of what is happening in the present moment when you are giving something of yourself to others, you gradually become aware of when giving takes too much out of you. You become more aware of a constrained and tight feeling when you are giving more than you should. You may become aware of a sense of resentment or exhaustion when you offer or agree to give something that will deplete you physically or mentally. With greater awareness of when you are giving too much, you will eventually learn how to set boundaries for how much you give. Setting these boundaries will lead to a sense of ease. Following this precept, you will find ways to give that increase your feelings of energy, joy and equanimity.

Meditating daily is the single most generous thing you can do. It is the most powerful way to contribute to world peace, the sustainability of our planet, the well-being of others and your own happiness. With daily meditation, each breath expands your capacity for understanding, generating creative solutions and taking action. When you meditate every day, you come to notice that your intentions and actions change, and you leave behind you a wake of loving interactions in your relationships.

Exercise with Precept 2: Death and Generosity

Imagine that you have died and that you are at your own memorial service. You have lived a long and fulfilling life. You experienced much happiness in your life. When you died, you were ready. Your loved ones—and there are many—are gathered for your memorial, and they are all saying how generous you were. Ask yourself the following three questions:

- What are people saying about the ways you shared yourself with others?

- What are people saying about ways you gave from your heart?

- What are people saying about ways you showed that you really cared?

Answer these questions as generously as you can. Think of the ways you have been loving, kind and generous. Most people when asked to do this exercise discover that their mind automatically goes to all the ways they are selfish, ungenerous or inadequate. This is a bad habit of mind which is not helpful.

When you have gathered one or two answers to a question, sit with the thoughts that arose. Let the ways you have been generous sink into your heart. Practice this exercise once a week for three months or more, once a day for two weeks, or every night before you go to sleep for the rest of your life. To reflect upon one's goodness prior to sleep every night is a fine practice and preparation for one's own death. In Thailand, this practice is understood to prepare you for the moment on your deathbed when you look back at your life and you encounter great vistas of your acts of kindness and generosity.

Traditional Precept 3: Refraining from Sexual Acts That Cause Harm

The traditional translation of the third precept is:

I undertake the training of the heart to refrain from sexual acts that cause harm.

Remember our primary impulses mentioned at the beginning of this chapter? At the most mammalian level, each time we encounter another being there are three fundamental questions, *Do I have to fight it? Can I eat it? Can I mate with it?*

Sexuality is a powerful force. In one sense, it is our prime directive. Without the mechanism of sexuality, humans would become extinct. Sexual impulses are normal. They can also be strong and easily overpower better judgment.

Have you ever made a fool of yourself because of your sexual longing? Have you ever made a complete mess of your life because of sexuality? Have you ever acted on your sexuality in some way that did not really fit with your ethics and morals? Almost everyone has. When conditions are lined up just so, even the most rational, balanced and loving person can do things for the sake of sexuality that they later regret.

The Buddha taught that until a person has some significant degree of awakening, they are capable of being swept into acting out unskillfully.

Some aspects of practicing this precept are easy. Rape or sexual harassment result in lasting physical and psychological harm to the victim. Basic restraint from such illegal behaviors is an obvious way to practice this precept, but the function of this precept is not limited to such extreme acts. It can provide guidance any time acting on sexual desire occurs.

One way to follow this precept is to be sure that the person with whom you are being sexual is truly giving consent and not harming themselves or others by violating their commitments. Another, less obvious, way to follow this precept is saying no when being sexual is not the right thing for you. The way in which you do not give consent should also do no harm. Treat the person with whom you do not want to be intimate kindly and with respect, and not as if they were a rapist or perpetrator—unless they are actually acting that way. Another way to follow this precept is to refrain from using your sexuality to distract or manipulate others.

This precept does not imply that sexuality is bad or wrong. It does not say *never be sexual* or *sexuality is unspiritual*. It guides us to become aware when sexuality arises in our lives and helps us to avoid doing harm to ourselves and others.

This precept can also be used as a guide for times in life when sexuality can be confusing. During the teen years, when the hormones are raging, young people are particularly vulnerable to acting sexually in ways that harm others and themselves. As parents, this precept can be helpful to guide a teenager who is navigating dating and physical intimacy. Today, the first forays for some teens into courtship are via apps. Young people use texting, Snapchat, Tinder or other apps for one-on-one conversations, and parents may not know anything about the app their teen is using. It is worth periodically searching online to discover the most popular apps for teens. Then, ask your teen if they have heard of one or another of these apps by name, and if so, ask them if they like it. Teenagers may like the anonymity of communicating through an app, but that can lead to using it in ways that cause harm. If you are on good terms with your teenager, guide them to ensure their messages reflect respectful and consensual content. You can talk with them about how they can use this precept on Snapchat or other apps.

In relationships where sexual and other intimacy needs are not being met, it can be confusing or difficult to follow this precept. Having an affair behind your partner's back is one way to use sexuality that causes harm. Withholding intimacy to punish or teach your partner a lesson is another. If you find yourself doing either of these things or some version of them, come back to this precept. Have the conversations you need to have and, if necessary, find an experienced couples' therapist to help you decide what to do to either bring intimacy back into your relationship, or skillfully part ways.

If you are withholding intimacy, it may be that a relationship has run its course, the chemistry was never there in the first place or you may be blaming your partner for something that has little or nothing to do with them. Much of the time, withholding sexuality is a symptom of another problem. If you are having an affair, or are about to, take the time to contemplate the full effect it will have on your partner, your children, your friends and family, colleagues and community. Maybe the person you are having the affair with is the right person for you and your other relationship has run its course, or there may be a problem in your relationship with your partner that needs the level of attention you are giving someone else. In both cases, as uncomfortable as it can be, sit with the circumstances of your situation and, if possible, talk with a teacher, therapist or a good friend about what is happening in your life.

There are two mental factors which serve to protect us. They are known as the great protectors. They are called *hiri* and *ottopa* in the Pali Canon, a collection of Buddhist scriptures. Hiri, moral shame, is the discomfort that emerges in a healthy mind when you've done something that causes harm to yourself or another person. This experience is very educational. It's easy to fall into toxic blame and self-hatred in modern Western culture. Skillful awareness of hiri teaches us to use the feeling of moral shame to guide us in upright behavior and not to punish ourselves. The second protecting mental factor is ottopa, moral dread. When we are mindful of our intentions, ottopa arises as we are about to make the same mistake that caused us moral shame (hiri) in the past. When following this precept and being mindful of the mental factors of hiri and ottopa, a strong resistance to having the same unpleasant experience of moral shame will arise when contemplating transgressing a precept. This can be instructive and liberating. Hiri and ottopa are helpful for all of the precepts.

Between my first and second marriage, I was in a thirteen-year partnership with a woman whom I truly loved. We shared the task of raising our five shared children. Sadly, our wounds were such that despite much effort, we were unable to find a way to be with each other in a loving way. We became stuck in a relationship that was no longer intimate or alive. Another relationship came between us as I became secretly involved with another woman, causing the long overdue breakup of our partnership. It happened in a way that brought a cascade of hurt to both of us and to our community. There was a lot of judgment, anger, shame and blaming. It was one of the darkest and most difficult times of my life.

That anguished time taught me the importance of the words *I undertake the training of the heart.* The precepts are similar to the laws of physics. Just as gravity results in objects falling to the earth, actions not in accord with the precepts lead to suffering. The precepts exist to guide us because we are fallible. They are aspirations that point us in the direction of happiness and away from suffering.

If you have had an affair or have a pattern of withholding intimacy in a relationship, in all likelihood you know well the harm that is caused from these kinds of sexual acts. You experienced the harm it has done to your own heart, to your partner, family, friends and community. Even so, this precept is not intended to be used as punishment. Holding yourself in compassion for the harm that you have caused is one step towards greater wisdom, which will help you follow the precept going forward.

Others, if they hear that you have not followed this precept, may feel compelled to punish you. Do not use this precept to join them in its misapplication for the purpose of punishment. Instead, work through your own grief, shame and self-hatred through meditation and talking with a teacher, therapist or good friend, so that you can come to a place of compassion, forgiveness and wisdom.

Positive Precept 3: Love, Relationship and Beauty

The positive interpretation of the third precept is:

I aspire to nurture love, relationship and beauty.

Creating and acting in the world is part of human nature. We are all manifestations of the creative impulse of life. You can follow this precept by using your life energy to create beauty and connection. It doesn't matter if you think of yourself as artistic or not. What matters is finding what you love to do and doing it with the intent of creating beauty. If you love to cook, cook with intent to create a beautiful meal that communicates your love. If you love to drive or hike, take your path in ways that are beautiful for you and others. If you love to talk or write, set an intention for your words to yield a sense of beauty.

You also can follow this precept by being loving with words and deeds. You can light up someone's day with a random act of kindness. If you are having a bad day, you can be kind to yourself by allowing yourself to retreat into a safe place, doing things that feel good and are healthy, and giving yourself a few moments or an hour for meditation.

Sexual energy is another expression of this life energy. If you have a partner with whom you are sexual, you can use this precept to guide you in how you make love. Following this precept, you bring your full attention to your beloved when you are embracing her or him. You can use this precept to guide you to make love mindfully, whether gently or exuberantly, with great love, joy, creativity and energy.

Exercise with Precept 3: Creating Beauty

Look for places where you can create beauty in your home, office, car or any other space you inhabit. If you don't think of yourself as good at decorating, don't let this stop you. Set an intention to surround yourself with beauty. Start with small areas and spread beauty throughout your life. Some ways to create beauty are to fill several vases with flowers and put them together on a table. You can create an altar to your ancestors with nicely framed pictures of your parents and grandparents, and a picture of yourself that you really like. In your medicine cabinet, arrange little knick-knacks, costume jewelry or other pretty things between the Band-Aids and medicines to make a pleasing display. If you have the space, make a display of your baby pictures and other childhood memorabilia in a drawer or cabinet so that when you open it you have something beautiful and pleasing to look at. These are just a few ideas for creating beauty in small spots in your home. There are many others. Give your heart full permission to make the effort to create beauty.

If you are in a relationship with a significant other, the next time you greet them, do so as if you are seeing the most splendid being for the first time. Greet them full of open and loving curiosity about everything about them and appreciate all the ways they are similar and different from you. When you find yourself slipping back into old patterns, notice this, and bring yourself back to open curiosity and appreciation.

Traditional Precept 4: Refraining from False and Harmful Speech

The traditional translation of the fourth precept is:

I undertake the training of the heart to refrain from harmful speech.

This precept guides us to refrain from gossip, lies, slander, idle chatter and verbal abuse, as well as any other way we use words in hurtful ways. It guides us to be mindful of our intent when we speak, and to be aware of the impact of our words on others. As awareness of your words' impact on yourself and others grows, you will find a feeling of liberty as you disavow harmful speech.

Giving up gossip can be hard. Gossiping is talking about someone when they're not present, usually with exaggerations or lies, and often entailing personal details. Ways to know you are gossiping are to ask yourself how you would feel if someone were saying the same things about you behind your back, or how it would be to say these same things in the presence of the person you are speaking about. Mostly, we gossip to create and maintain bonds with other people. It can give us a sense of belonging to an in-group. Gossip is harmful because it isolates and excludes the subject of the gossip, creates a false sense of separateness and superiority, and because the words that are spoken are often mean and damaging. Another reason gossip is harmful is that it displaces opportunities for connection based on shared values and interests. It can be a way to avoid intimacy and honesty.

Gossip is common in many work places. Giving it up can have major ramifications on your relationships. People may feel threatened by you or resent you for not gossiping with them anymore. As you refrain from gossip, it may feel like there is nothing interesting to talk about. Uncomfortable silence may come between you and your colleagues. Instead, try to find things you have in common to talk about that don't involve other people. Give your colleagues genuine compliments and appreciation. Telling someone what you admire about them or praising them for something you thought they did well can rebuild connections with people at work.

Sometimes we talk about someone who isn't present because we care about them and want to help them. This is useful, and sometimes even essential. Other times, we triangulate and speak about someone who isn't present to avoid talking about what is really going on with someone in the present space. In this way, we may be avoiding intimacy while trying to maintain some connection.

This is a common experience with couples with kids. Their conversations can become exclusively about their children. Then, the last child leaves home. For years, they didn't share what was going on in their own lives, hearts and minds. They rarely or never talked about what they had in common besides their children. They consistently avoided conflict, and with an empty nest they find a tense chasm has grown between them. They have nothing to talk about, and nothing in common.

If you are in a relationship, and there are children, try to refrain from speaking about them for a day or two. Note how much silence results between the two of you. Seek ways to communicate about what is happening in your life that is about you and not your children, and about what you have in common with your partner that has nothing to do with them.

This precept also applies to the subtle ways we use words that cause harm. Have you ever been in the situation when someone said something that seemed like it was helpful or appreciative, but left you feeling ashamed, insecure, worthless or deflated? You may not be able to put your finger on exactly what it was that led to those feelings—maybe the tone, body language, timing or the arrangement of words. Think back to the last time you can remember feeling this way. It doesn't matter if you don't remember exactly what was said. Once the feelings arise, notice where they occur in your body. Notice the thoughts that arise with these feelings. Next, ask yourself if you have ever used words in a subtle way to make someone feel badly about themselves, intentionally or unintentionally. Hold that memory in mind and ask yourself what your intent was when you spoke. If it was to harm the other person, ask yourself why you wanted to harm them. If you did intend to harm the other person, a feeling of hiri (moral shame) probably arises. This is a good sign, and instructive in helping you follow this precept.

Harmful speech also occurs in the form of internal negative self-talk and self-hatred. This is unconscious conditioned behavior, learned in childhood. It is essentially a bad habit of the mind. I call it malware. This precept helps us become aware when the malware kicks in and the mind speaks in self-hating ways. From now on, notice when you are experiencing negative self-talk. The most powerful intervention is to simply become aware of this.

As you become more aware, you will be more capable of replacing the negative self-talk with skillful speech. You can use the refrain from Jack Kornfield's book *The Wise Heart*: " I aspire to love and accept myself exactly as I am in this moment." Pause after you say the refrain. Note what arises. Repeat the refrain and note again what arises. Over time, you will notice that feelings of compassion for yourself eventually emerge when negative self-talk kicks in.

Positive Precept 4: Speak to Create Happiness, Harmony and Understanding

The positive interpretation of the fourth precept is:

I aspire to use speech to create happiness, harmony and understanding.

We are not born knowing how to use words to create happiness, harmony and understanding. We are, however, born with the ability to express our feelings and needs directly. As babies, we cried out with small squeals or loud wails, and eventually our needs were taken care of. We let our feelings and needs be known directly and simply. As we grew up we learned to hide our true feelings behind words, judgments and criticisms. Imagine how unhelpful it would be if instead of crying the baby said, *Hey you, get over here and change my diaper. You never pay attention to me and are so pathologically selfish.* When we speak like that as adults, we rarely get our needs met. We engender resentment and usually start a fight. These learned and ingrained patterns of communicating leave us feeling isolated, misunderstood and miserable.

In order to speak skillfully, we must become conscious of how we speak. I have studied non-violent communication (NVC) for over a decade. NVC is a method of conscious, compassionate speech developed by Marshall Rosenberg in which we learn to communicate empathically. We learn how to articulate our feelings and needs and to make effective present moment requests. Our feelings can be heard and our needs met when we learn how to express them in ways that do not drive the other person away. In intimate relationship we can learn to talk about what's happening in the present moment without conflating it with the past or future. I believe Buddha would have approved of

Marshall Rosenberg's compassionate communication methodology. I highly recommend learning and practicing non-violent communication.

Buddha taught five questions you can use to check whether what you are about to say will create happiness, harmony and understanding. They are:

1. Is what I am about to say truthful?

2. Is what I am about to say helpful?

3. Is what I am about to say necessary?

4. Is what I am about to say kind?

5. Is it the right time to say it?

As difficult as it can be, if the answer to any of these questions is no, then remain silent. This is a very challenging undertaking because sometimes we are very attached to our views and opinions. When we feel an urgency to say something unskillfully but don't speak, we can see how we cause our own suffering by wanting things to be different from the way they are. Exercising restraint in this way strengthens us and we become better communicators when it is the right time to speak.

This precept should not be taken to mean that you should always hold your tongue and suffer through anything. Instead, it guides you to speak at times and in ways that are helpful to you and others. Most interpersonal conflict can be healthily resolved when we wait for the right time to speak our truth, and then speak more skillfully.

Exercise with Precept 4: Self-Talk

Set an intention to observe the self-judging mind with compassion and acceptance, and to free yourself from identification with negative self-talk. Next time you observe the mind thinking in self-critical ways, notice the old pattern of malware when it starts. Note, *Oh, there it is again, the negative self-talk happening.* The more often you wake up to these old patterns after they arise, the more you develop your capacity to notice them as they are arising. Over time, you will notice them right as they emerge into consciousness and you will be able to nip them in the bud. This is the wise effort of mindfulness. By neither resisting nor attaching to negative self-talk, it will gradually fade away.

Traditional Precept 5: Refraining from Intoxicants

The traditional translation of the last precept is:

I undertake the training of the heart to refrain from using intoxicants.

Remember the First Noble Truth? There is pain. Just to be alive means suffering a litany of pains: birth, sickness, old age, decay and death; being with people you do not want to be with, not being with people you want to be with; having experiences you do not want to have, and not having experiences you do want to have. Life is hard.

We do all kinds of things to intoxicate ourselves because ordinary consciousness can be pretty grim. In his book *The Natural Mind*, Andrew Weil hypothesized that ordinary reality is so difficult that we must have altered states. We have found many ways to create various altered states. We dance. We ski. We listen to music. We read a book or watch a sunset. There are many things we do to create an altered state. But not all the ways we alter our consciousness are skillful.

Using intoxicants is an unskillful way of creating an altered state. One of the reasons it is unskillful is that the use of intoxicants has a price. The more you use them, the more the body adapts to them. To get to the same altered state, you have to increase your dose. After some time, you need the substances in order to feel normal, and when your body is without the substance, you feel bad. This is addiction, and we easily become addicted.

For many years in my early adulthood, I self-medicated with marijuana. In my social world it was a normal thing to do. I was meditating for an hour or two a day and smoking marijuana on a daily basis, sometimes more than once a day. Spiritually, it was like having one foot on the gas and the other on the brake. In retrospect the harmfulness of this habitual use is clear, but at the time, the phenomenon of denial kept that realization obscured. In Buddhism, denial is represented by the word *ignorance*. Two events occurred back to back in my life that resulted in my waking up to my habit of intoxication.

My wife and I went to the symphony one evening and got stoned in the car before we went into the hall. I experienced a profound contraction of consciousness and the arising of anxiety. My old friend marijuana, that had previously provoked what had seemed like expanded states of consciousness, had turned on me. At this point in my practice I had developed sufficient mindfulness that I could not deny the unpleasant shift. Soon after the night at the symphony, my four-year-old son walked into a room where my wife and I were secretly smoking marijuana with friends. He looked at me and said, *Daddy, what are you doing, you don't smoke.* The veil of denial fell away. It came clear to me that I had been blurring myself out for years.

Why was I doing that?

I resolved to quit smoking. What emerged with the cessation of using marijuana was deep depression and anxiety. Issues of intimacy and self-worth also arose. It became clear that using intoxicants had been a way of avoiding looking at myself. With therapy, antidepressant medication and mindfulness practice I learned to function better in my life and to face some of the challenges of embracing and unwinding some of my early wounding and trauma.

The fact is, we all have addictive and compulsive behaviors because life is painful. In my Dharma talks, I sometime ask the question, *Do you do something on a regular basis that you know you would be better off if you did not?* Almost every person in the room raises their hand. Why is this?

It is human nature.

All addictive and compulsive patterns have to do with avoiding something. The common ingredient in all addictions is denial. To awaken from our addictions is to confront the grief, depression, anger, loneliness, fear and resentments that we have been avoiding.

Some of our addictive and compulsive behaviors are socially encouraged. Some can be healthy if managed well, such as exercising, meditating, attending support or recovery groups. Some are illegal. Some are deadly. It makes sense to be skillful about which addictive and compulsive behaviors we choose to do.

The first step for skillful action towards addictive and compulsive behavior is to assess your patterns. Do you spend hours every night watching TV to avoid feelings of loneliness? Do you compulsively give gifts as a way of feeling valuable and worthwhile? Do you read all the time, even when you are eating? Do you leave the radio or music going to distract yourself from sadness or exhaustion? Do you check your phone a hundred times a day? Brain scans show that when the phone sends out notifications, for most of us there is a little release of dopamine. That beep, ring or chirp is giving you a little release of pleasure. It says, *You are wanted. You exist. You are noticed.*

The next step is to practice the art of loving yourself. One of my esteemed teachers, Ajahn Sumedho, the senior Western monk in the Thai Forest Tradition, describes love this way: *Love means there is room for everything.* In order to transcend our unhealthy addictive habits, we must come to perceive ourselves—our thoughts, feelings and behaviors—clearly and without judgment. Learning to love yourself is a process. The meditation practice on lovingkindness is a useful tool for this. You can listen to recorded lovingkindness meditations by a teacher whose voice conveys love to you and by practicing lovingkindness meditations. (You can find recorded lovingkindness meditations at portlandinsight.org/node/25)

The third step is to replace unhealthy activities with healthy ones and build your community with like-minded, healthy people. Aspire to make your meditation practice, instead of your addictive behavior, your go-to activity for relief from suffering. It is challenging for most people to change habits because old relationships based in addiction tend to lock them into harmful behaviors. It is crucial to create new friendships. Find a community to meditate with or have at least one Dharma friend with whom you meditate, read books and discuss your practice. Refuge Recovery (refugerecovery.org) offers a healthy Dharma-based community for recovery from addiction. In addition, there are 12-step groups, treatment centers and therapists who specialize in addiction issues.

Positive Precept 5: Mindfulness, Compassion and Equanimity

The positive interpretation of the fifth precept is:

I aspire to cultivate mindfulness, compassion and wisdom.

To follow the positive interpretation of the fifth precept, we work to replace our old addictive habits with habits of being present, awake and compassionate in every moment and activity of life.

Exercise with Precept 5: Intoxicants

Ask yourself, *When and why do I use intoxicants?* You can carry out mindfulness research in your life to discover the answers. When you find yourself about to indulge, pause. Pay attention inwardly, and become aware of the uncomfortable mood, emotion, thoughts or mental state you are seeking to avoid. Pause for one or two minutes before taking that drink, smoke or screen hit. If you do indulge the craving, stay mindful and see what the effect is. Each time you do this, you are cultivating more mindfulness and confronting denial. This will change your relationship with your intoxicant.

Following the Precepts

I hope that this chapter will inspire you to make use of the precepts in your life. I also hope you have noted that there is no judgment in the precepts. There is nothing in them that says, *You're a bad person* when you break any of these precepts. Change comes about through insight and compassion, not through violence or coercion in any form.

Often it is best not to try to follow all the precepts at the same time if they are new to you. You can't fix everything at the same time. Instead, start with just one. If you aren't sure which one, decide where you're making your life miserable because you aren't following a precept, then start there.

Habitual behaviors take a while to notice, suffer with and change. With all the precepts, remember the saying, *progress not perfection*. Learning to act in accordance with the precepts is a process that takes time.

Be gentle with yourself.

7

Challenging Mental States

IF WE COULD SEE what is going on inside each other's minds, we would all be stricken with compassion. We would see how much everyone longs to be loved and suffers from old trauma and the pain caused by an out-of-control mind.

Buddha's teachings offer a direct path to diminish and ultimately eliminate suffering. We learn to observe suffering and its causes from a more and more spacious and non-judgmental perspective.

When I first came to meditation, I practiced with a desperate longing *to get enlightened and just get out of here.* I wanted to transcend pain, suffering and loss and just vanish in a puff of smoke. The tension and fruitlessness of this view has become clear. The path to freedom and happiness does not lead up, up and away. It goes down, down and in. Opening into awareness allows accepting more and more of ourselves. In time, mindfulness embraces all aspects of our being, including the parts we have denied and projected onto others. It's a bit like archaeology. The more we explore inwardly the more we learn about ancient buried thoughts and feelings. We reveal depths of previously unknown thoughts and feelings as well as riches of love and compassion.

Difficult Mental States

The First Noble Truth describes our situation brilliantly: suffering really exists. It is ubiquitous and inherent in being born. Nobody is excluded. We experience birth, sickness, old age, decay and death. In addition, we experience being with people we would prefer not to be with and the absence of those we long for. We also have many experiences we would prefer not to have and do not have experiences we long for. (See Chapter 5: The Eightfold Path, or the Path to Happiness for reminders about the Four Noble Truths).

Difficult mental states often arise. This is natural. Everybody has feelings of anger, hatred, disgust, loneliness, fear, anxiety and sadness. Some of us are not aware of our feelings or the extent of them when they arise or are present. It can be very helpful to learn how to identify your own feelings. There are a few feelings common to humankind that tend to come up when things are difficult. They are:

- Loneliness, isolation, disconnection

- Anger, hatred, self-hatred, rejection, disgust, contempt

- Fear, anxiety, panic, worry, confusion

- Depression, hopelessness, fatigue, sadness, numbness

The following two questions and instructions were devised to help you recognize the extent of a difficult mental state. Are any of the feelings listed here in you right now? If so, how do you know? Write down with a word or sentence how you know the feeling is present. Look for where they are experienced in your body. For some feelings, it may be a sense of hollowness in the chest, a heaviness in the belly, or a tightness in the neck and shoulders. You might become aware of a dull pain in a certain area of your body, or the onset of a familiar stomach or headache. An overwhelming sense of urgency to do something else might arise. You might find yourself numb. If you are not experiencing a difficult feeling right now, come back to this exercise next time you are, or reflect upon the last time you did experience a difficult mental state. Once you have done this experiment while in a difficult state, remind yourself that your experience is part of the human condition. The miraculous teaching of Buddha was not that we can avoid these difficult states, but that we can learn to deal with them, so we do not suffer.

Developing Capacity Through Awareness

One way to develop your capacity for dealing wisely with challenging mental states is to observe them when you are meditating. You have probably already noticed that when you meditate you encounter many challenges. You may sit down to meditate and very quickly experience worry, sadness or anger. Sometimes the feelings or thoughts are so strong it becomes intolerable to meditate a moment more, so you get up and busy yourself so you don't have to experience that mental state. When this happens, instead of chastising yourself for not being able to sit with your difficult mental state, congratulate yourself for identifying it. Note also that your mental state is a normal human experience. Next time you sit down to meditate, when the difficult mental state arises, note its arising. Stay with it if you can, and again congratulate yourself that you recognized it.

Over time, you will notice the arising and passing of mental states. You will still have the feelings and thoughts. Your body will still experience a tenseness in the neck and shoulders, a tidal wave of desire to do something else, or any of the other things that happen in your body when difficult mental states arise. And you will develop the capacity for awareness of the arising of these inner experiences. In developing this capacity to notice their arising, you expand your capacity to deal with them wisely.

Developing Capacity Through Pain

It may seem odd, but one way to build your capacity for dealing with challenging mental states is through physical pain meditation. You can practice with a pain that is a frequent visitor, like a backache, sore shoulder or an injury, or by sitting up very straight if your usual posture is slumped. If your posture has been causing you pain, sit in a position that will not cause further harm, or shift positions as often as you need to in order to keep yourself from causing more harm to your body. Sit in a chair, if sitting on the floor would damage your body. I've known some people who meditated in a painful position without moving for a long time and ended up with permanent damage. Don't do this. It is the same for other aspects of your health. For example, if you are prone to migraines take your medicine, and then sit or lie and embrace whatever you experience. Be gentle with yourself, and never use meditation in a way that would cause harm.

Knowing you will experience harmless physical pain during meditation, you can begin with the intention of paying attention to the breath. At the beginning of meditation, the wandering mind arises and carries you away. You bring your attention back to the breath. Your mind wanders again. Perhaps the thoughts that arise are pleasant. Maybe they are unpleasant. You bring your attention back to the breath. Then the pain comes. You bring your mind back to the breath and, for just a moment, experience relief. It hurts again, this time worse. Again, you bring your mind back to the breath and again, a moment of relief, but the relief is quickly broken. Now it really hurts.

What should you do? Maybe you decide it is time to stop meditating or to change positions. You naturally want to get away from the pain. The skillful thing to do is intentionally let go of the breath as your meditation object and take the pain as your meditation object. Notice that an unpleasant state has arisen. Attend closely to the sensations of pain. Notice the mind's response, *I hate this. Why is this so hard? Why is this happening to me?* Sometimes the pain abates. Sometimes the pain intensifies. Every time it arises, intensifies, abates or passes, notice it. Notice also that there is pain and that there is resistance to the pain. Notice that this resistance is in the mind.

You will come to know from these experiences that suffering comes from an unenforceable rule: *There should not be pain.*

Working with pain is counterintuitive. Because you are a normal mammal, and escaping pain was essential for your survival; you will want to move or flee somehow. Ask yourself the question, *Is this pain somehow damaging my body?* If it is, then mindfully move to a new position. If it's not, this pain offers a golden opportunity for learning about the Four Noble Truths and the end of suffering.

If this is a moment in which you are willing to explore the nature of pain and suffering and the relief from suffering, turn your attention toward the actual experience of pain. Take the sensations in your body as your meditation object and get as intimate and close to them as you possibly can. Notice the resistance to doing this. Notice that muscles may tighten up. Become aware of the thoughts and emotions that arise. Sometimes there is a tendency toward panic or hatred as the mind looks for a way out.

Once you are well established in bearing this pain consciously, you are in a perfect position to observe the way the mind craves escape from unpleasant sensations. This is your unenforceable rule: *I shouldn't suffer this discomfort; it is dangerous to suffer this discomfort; it is not fair that I'm experiencing this.* At some point as you consciously suffer the actual pain and the responses to it, something strange will occur. The craving—the Second Noble Truth—will stop, and the pain—the First Noble Truth—may stay the same or dissipate. This quenching of suffering arises from extinguishing the demand that something be different than it is. This is what Buddha referred to as nirvana. Rather than mistaking nirvana for a form of heaven or another world to escape to, it is wise to understand it as the quenching of craving, the diminution and eventual extinction of the suffering caused by greed, hatred and ignorance of reality.

If you continue to practice in this way you may discover that the suffering returns, then disappears. We learn in order to accept life on its own terms, including when there is pain. In so doing we free ourselves to live life more fully.

You will gradually develop your capacity to deal with unpleasant experiences, both physical and emotional. First you learn to notice when they arise. Then you learn to notice their arising and passing. You learn that they are normal human experiences. You learn to allow them to be what they are. You learn to soften to your own difficult mental states, and to those of others. You learn to open your heart to yourself and others.

The simple noticing of the arising of the pain and the mind's response is what builds your capacity for dealing with difficult mental states. The noticing is the remedy to suffering. I think this is the greatest discovery that ever occurred to humanity.

You will develop compassion as you learn to embrace and accept the pain and difficulties that arise in your life. You will not have to turn away and distract yourself. Simultaneously, you will naturally begin to see the pain and suffering in those around you. This is a natural evolution as you become a person of psychological and spiritual maturity.

Depression

Many people will go through at least one period of depression in their lives. Some experience quite a lot of depression, which sometimes lasts for years. Sometimes depression arises due to life conditions, sometimes from biochemistry, and often from a combination. It's a common human experience.

Depression is very convincing. When it is present it makes us believe *This is the real me, I have always been depressed. Yesterday I was joyful and dancing but that was not the real me. That was a fake. Depression is the real me.*

I spent decades of my life depressed, including many years while I was learning and teaching the Dharma. For ten years of my life, I took antidepressant medication. Psychotherapy and medication have been extremely helpful to me. The circumstances of my life have changed a lot since those times and depression is mostly absent, but if I were to find myself struggling with depression again, I would spend more time in silence, withdraw into retreat for a while, seek the support of therapy. If necessary, I would once again take medication

I have also worked with many people suffering from depression. I usually advise a good mental health therapist, cardiovascular exercise, and proper use of the appropriate antidepressants along with practicing mindfulness. One of the misconceptions that's arisen in the spiritual world is that meditation or other spiritual practices will cure anything, and you should never take medications. When depression is severe and disrupting your life, the right medication and help from a good therapist can be a wise thing to do. Exercise and a good diet are also potent antidepressants. Walking for half an hour a day can have a powerful effect on your mood or tendency towards depression. Walk fast enough to get your heart beating. You do not have to push yourself too hard, just enough to increase your heart rate. (If you have heart problems or other health issues, check with your doctor first.) Eating enough protein and five or six portions of fruits or vegetables a day is also important.

You may already exercise regularly and eat a good diet. Perhaps you are seeing a therapist or have already spent a few years in therapy. Then something happens to trigger depression, or maybe you just wake up with that familiar dull, heavy, awful state. That feeling that you are the depression is so very convincing. You may have practiced mindfulness enough to know that everything is impermanent and the feeling will pass, or you know intellectually that you are not the depression, but this knowledge does not feel helpful in the face of depression.

What should you do? The wise thing is to turn your meditative attention towards the experience that you call depression. Make the depression your object of meditation.

Start your meditation by asking yourself, *How do I know I am depressed?* Notice the thoughts and shades of feelings that arise. Note each thought or feeling by stating it to yourself. Perhaps you notice a teary feeling and desire to not be alive. Note to yourself, *A teary feeling has arisen; the mental state of not wanting to be alive has arisen.* Attend to that, and when it intensifies, abates and eventually passes, notice this. Notice the next mental state that arises. Perhaps feelings of self-loathing arise. Perhaps it is difficult to think, and the head feels heavy, dull and like it is full of cement. Notice these feelings, thoughts and body sensations, and note their arising and passing. Notice that it is not just mind. It involves the body. Notice how they manifest in your body.

When we approach depression with mindfulness, we come into awareness. We go beyond the story, *I am depressed* and identifying with the feeling of that state. We are noticing the thoughts, feelings and body sensations. We become the eyes from the image in the first chapter of this book.

It does not necessarily mean that the state changes. It does means that your identification with the state lessens.

Sometimes practicing mindfulness of depression results in it changing, sometimes it does not, but awareness of the depression is the intervention. Practicing mindfulness like this can help you know at an experiential level that you are not the depression.

Anger

Anger is another challenging mental state. Anger is there because it helped us survive. When we come under attack, anger mobilizes us quickly. Anger can be useful when used skillfully.

Our relationship to anger is conditioned by our family of origin, the culture we live in and many life experiences. We may have been trained that good little boys and girls never get angry. Some of us have been trained to use anger to get our way.

When anger is blooming in the mind and body, stomping meditation is often more functional than sitting meditation. Stomping meditation uses up some of the body chemistry. Next time you are feeling angry, try an intentional and conscious fast walking or stomping meditation. At first, walk fast and be aware of the legs pounding. Watch the mind filled with enemy imaging. Watch the story of the anger. Watch the justification. Watch the phases of the storm. Notice how long it takes for the mind to begin to calm down. When the storm begins to subside, and the body chemistry is calming down, sit down and take the anger as your meditation object.

What is it? How do you know you are angry? What is happening in the mind? Where does it reside in the body? When anger is present, there is often a tensing of your dominant arm in an impulse to strike. There is also sometimes a clenching of the jaw. This is the impulse to bite. Notice this.

When the body's system gets engaged with anger, enemy images usually come up. Sometimes these are directed towards the self. Sometimes they are directed towards others. Conclusions are made. Decisions are come to. There is the diagnosing of others or of the self. The rightness of these thoughts is very convincing. Notice all of this without judgment. If self-judgment arises just observe that, too. You don't have to get rid of any of these experiences. In fact, they all arise and pass away on their own.

With mindfulness, you notice the state of anger, and you go beyond the story, *I am angry.* Mindfulness breaks the identification of yourself as the feeling of anger. When you meditate with anger as your meditation object, you train yourself to be mindful of your anger when you are not meditating. This does not mean that the state changes. What changes is your relationship to the state. If you practice mindfulness of anger, eventually wisdom and compassion will arise in unexpected and liberating ways.

Our Common Experiences

Challenging mental states are an inevitable part of the human experience. We experience depression, anger, hatred, anxiety, fear and many other difficult emotions. We all suffer sometimes.

Mindfulness meditation builds our capacity to accept everything and to deal with wisdom, compassion and love with our own and other people's difficult states. We learn to accept with grace what we cannot change, and to skillfully change what we can.

Oddly enough, the fastest way to change something is to accept it as it is. Let's say you have a difficult feeling or thought. The task is to accept the difficult feeling or thought arising as it is, and neither push it away or give into it. Notice, *Here it is, this is how it is flowering. This is the moment of this feeling or thought.*

The pattern arises and falls away.

It comes and goes.

Over time it diminishes.

Eventually, it self-extinguishes.

You find you can just be, observing reality as it is.

You now know how to cultivate mindfulness in sitting meditation and in all the activities of daily life. You understand how to turn toward the suffering that arises in your life and transform it into wisdom, love and compassion. You are likely more conscious of the behaviors you choose and how they influence your sense of well-being and connection with others. I hope that you feel more confident that you can embrace your life more intimately, and that you are engaged in the lifetime process of loving yourself in all your complexity and imperfection. I also hope that you are finding yourself happier, more content and able to connect with others in the ways you would like to.

I have found regular meditation to be essential on my journey. I hope it is helpful to you in a similar way. If you sit in meditation for one hour a day, it will profoundly change your life. If you sit for twenty minutes a day, you will soon see the difference. If you take one minute to pay attention to your breath a day, you are on the path. Every hour, every moment, every breath counts. Every thought, every feeling, every action counts. It all counts. Practice now with everything that is.

Thirty-Three Thousand Feet

People sleep, watch videos,
play games on screens and sip at wine.
Flying West over snow covered mountains.
A chasm opened, or perhaps just revealed itself
with a taxi goodbye kiss.
That moment of looking away
it's always the same.
Here, and then not here.
Those moments that we actually have,
when we can touch, hear, see,
and smell one another other
are all we really have.
The stakes are high aren't they?
Either we connect and love one another now
or not at all.

—ROBERT BEATTY

Robert Beatty is a member of the first wave of Theravada Buddhist Teachers who brought the Dharma from Asia in the 1970's. He is devoted to helping others discover the profound ways Buddhist practices can transform one's life, reduce suffering and create happiness. Robert's meditation journey began in India 1972. He has studied with teachers in Burma, India and the US and traces his teaching lineage through Ruth Denison, who named him a Dharma successor in 1982. He is the founder of the Portland Insight Meditation Community where he is the guiding teacher. Robert leads retreats in British Columbia, Washington and Oregon. He uses silence, humor, movement, poetry and drumming to teach meditation for everyday life, including intimate relationships, parenting, and work. Learn more about Robert Beatty at www.robertbeatty.com and www.portlandinsight.org.

Laura Musikanski is the executive director of the Happiness Alliance (happycounts.org), one of the first nonprofits to provide tools and resources for a well-being-based economy to communities. She is the co-author of several books including the *Happiness Policy Handbook* and *Happiness, Well-being and Sustainability: A Course in Systems Change.*

Made in the USA
Las Vegas, NV
14 December 2020

13296284R00085